What others are sayin I0073894

ADVICE FROM A RISK DETECTIVE

"Annie Searle's new book, 'Advice from a Risk Detective,' is a 'must read' for everyone. Her insights as an operational risk executive translated to everyday life help the reader know how to manage their own risks at home, at school, at work, on the internet and on the road. The checklists are invaluable. Buy one for yourself as well as for your loved ones!"

Catherine A. Allen
Chairman and CEO
The Santa Fe Group

"Annie Searle takes a down-to-earth approach to addressing the range of risks that confront us at home, at school, work, on the road and online. She shares a personal perspective and history that enlivens and enriches what is too often a 'check list' mantra. There is no hype or unrealistic complexity here, just actionable insights that offer tremendous value to all."

Bill Raisch
Founding Director, InterCEP
New York University

"Don't be daunted by the innumerable risks of modern life. In this updated and handy reference book, Annie Searle serves as your personal risk consultant, providing practical ideas for identifying and reducing risks faced in situations like natural disasters or taking a new job. The reader can readily apply the material using her concrete checklists, advice and sources for more information. The general public and risk managers alike will find this refreshing approach a useful and accessible tool for protecting themselves, their employees and their families."

Brian Tishuk
General Counsel
FS-ISAC

"Chock-full of practical suggestions to manage risk at home, school, work, and on-the-go."

Dr. Kevin C. Desouza
Author
Intrapreneurship: Managing Ideas within Your Organization

ADVICE FROM A
RISK DETECTIVE

ANNIE SEARLE

Tautegory Press
Seattle, Washington

Printed in the United States of America
Tautegory Press, Seattle, Washington
USA Library of Congress Control Number: 2019912214
ISBN: 978-1-7334390-0-8

Cover design by Jesse Brown
Book design by Marie Williams Chant
Unless otherwise noted, photographs by Annie Searle

Many people have made this book possible, and I thank them all. Several figure more prominently for their ideas and support. In particular, for the first edition, I would like to thank Lauren Du Graf for seeing what could make this a better book; Emily Oxenford Hayes for masterful technical support; Jesse Brown for his design of the book; and editor Molly Martin for her keen eye. With the second edition, I would like to thank Devin Luco for a close reading of the text, and for his contributions. For this third edition, I should like to thank the hundreds of students I've taught about risk since 2012. Finally, my thanks to the two men who offer unwavering support of my work, Leroy F. Searle and James H.S. Searle.

TABLE OF CONTENTS

Introduction

This book will show you how to do it.[1]

I've been a risk detective most of my life.

I was hired at age twelve with a child-labor permit to be the lifeguard for the wading pool in the small Iowa town where I grew up — a fair amount of risk, since children under five years old love to run on wet concrete and are prone to fall and hit their heads. Over the years, I moved up to the regular pool and became a swimming instructor. Mornings were devoted to teaching kids and adults how to swim so that they would not have to be rescued. Lifeguarding in the afternoon and evening required constant scans of the environment and occasional rescues of swimmers in trouble.

1 This World War II poster was created in 1939 by the British Ministry of Information, in case of invasion. It was never published during the war. (Fair use, no copyright.)

The more training I had, the more confident I became that I could help people who might be in danger. I worked at the Buffalo Center Swimming Pool for seven summers, until I started my sophomore year in college — and the expertise I gained in incident management and safety training is central to some of the work I do today.

Part of my interest in teaching people how to stay out of trouble and solving thorny problems must surely have come from an earlier interest in Nancy Drew and Hardy Boys mystery novels.[2] I've been an active observer — gathering evidence, finding patterns or missing pieces, and solving puzzles or problems — ever since.

I learned to become a formal observer of others' behavior in graduate school, as a psychiatric-hospital worker on the night shift, where we actually "charted" patients' behavior. Though I was studying for two college literature degrees, my recreational reading repertoire included authors who had created classic analytical detectives, such as CID Inspector Roderick Alleyn (Ngaio Marsh), Commander Adam Dalgliesh (P.D. James) and Nero Wolfe (Rex Stout). After graduate school I worked on a daily newspaper, then in public broadcasting and the visual arts. Later, I helped found and then led Delphi Computers & Peripherals, a company that built computer-hardware platforms to drive legal, medical, biotechnical, and business innovation against complex customer requirements. We won a num-

---

2 The Nancy Drew Mystery Stories were first published in 1930 by Grosset and Dunlap. The original 56 stories were written by various people under the pseudonym of Carolyn Keene. The first 17 volumes of the Hardy Brothers series were written by Leslie McFarlane under the pseudonym of Franklin B. Dixon, starting in 1927.

ber of awards because we listened carefully to our customers and then delivered cutting-edge solutions that included solving a puzzle or two along the way.

I moved on to the world of banking in 1999, initially as a technology architect to build intranet and internet platforms. I went on to create a business-intelligence operation at Washington Mutual — our version of a detective agency — that could research and benchmark technology and innovation for the sixth-largest bank in the country against its key competitors. Over ten years, working with great teams, I was able to lay down a record for taking apart and rebuilding complex yet troubled programs. I spent eight of those years as a senior executive in charge of company-wide operational-risk programs for business continuity, crisis management, some elements of IT security, and all of audit and regulatory programs for technology. The bank loaned me to work on a variety of national projects that brought together academic, public-sector and private-sector perspectives.

I left banking in 2009 to start my own risk research and consulting firm. It was important to me to set up a private practice where I would never be bored and where I could continue to solve hard problems, especially those that seemed unsolvable. Like Delphi Computers & Peripherals, Annie Searle & Associates LLC (ASA) partners with a wide variety of businesses and organizations. From 2009 to 2015, the work involved identifying gaps in strategic plans and operational-risk programs, then building roadmaps to fix or close the highest-risk gaps. Since 2012, ASA's Institute for Risk and Innovation has published risk-related research and provided pro-bono services to several public institutions. ASA's aims parallel my own interests — to reduce the amount of risk in a variety of situations or environments by making solid plans and taking reasonable precautions. In my spare time, I continue to read great detective novels by contemporary authors such as Elizabeth George, Daniel Silva, and John Le Carre. It's not light reading but it offsets the darker issues that I think and write about professionally. Such reading always reminds me how many ways we can approach a problem, find the anomaly, recognize the pattern, gap or outlier — and then solve the problem.

This book springs out of a desire to simplify what I know and reach a larger audience than I do in private practice. It's a refinement of materials used for years to help businesses manage their risks. And I'm relatively certain that my ongoing love of detective novels will shine through as well. Like those novels, this book has a beginning, middle, and end — and creating it has been rather like putting together the pieces of a complex puzzle called "Risks in Life."

Learning to identify risks and making a plan to handle them reassures us and is not as difficult as it might first seem. The essence of this approach to life can be summarized in the World War II poster at the beginning of this introduction: "Keep Calm and Carry On."

England was never invaded, so the poster was never used during the war, but the words resonate with us today and the poster is reprinted widely. Even if economic and financial risk, for example, seem elevated over several years, calmness and perseverance are possible if we have plans that allow life and work to go forward. This book is divided into five sections: The first chapter deals with home safety, prudent management of domestic risks, and how to live without power or technology if necessary during a disaster. The second chapter examines types of risks for children from the moment you identify caregivers to the moment your children graduate from college. The third chapter looks at personal risk and independence in the workplace. The fourth chapter discusses your digital identity and the controls you can set up to protect yourself online. The fifth chapter deals with risks to manage while on the road, traveling in and around the world.

Taking risks is an essential part of personal growth. While in some cases we might try to eliminate a risk, what we are generally looking to do is manage it in such a way as to allow us to carry on without losing momentum.

This book will show you how to create simple plans and provide for a reasonable level of personal safety. I have tried to make a better book than one that simply scares you or increases your anxiety over a variety of "What if?" scenarios that you might not have considered.

Being aware means that it is possible to identify risks and make a plan. Being prepared means having more control over the outcome of events. I don't identify all the risks or all the plans that one can make. I do discuss what is reasonable rather than what is possible. And I'm not selling any products or solutions.

Acting on most of these precautions does not take a lot

of time, but rather simple steps that should work equally well for those who worry that something bad is about to happen, and for those who don't usually think twice about their failure to plan.

We still have to actively observe the world around us, but it's possible to live our lives in both physical and virtual worlds, fully engaged, part of a larger community with eyes wide open and plans well-made.

May 2013

In the several years since I wrote the first edition of this book, the world has changed, so I have added material to the original four chapters as appropriate, especially in the chapter that deals with online risks.

I have also added an entirely new chapter dealing with personal risks "at school," beginning at the moment you put your child in someone else's care. It has been a difficult chapter to finish since the mass shooting in the Newtown, Connecticut, school late in 2012, where most of the risk management practices I would recommend had already been in place, including training and drills. I have not been able to put the children or their parents out of mind as I worked; and, indeed, I wondered, from time to time, if it would be simpler to drop the new chapter. Who among us is qualified to give advice to other parents? But I hope that chapter is of use to readers.

August 2019

This third edition updates all material and adds commentary that springs from maintaining both a public speaking and publishing role while teaching as a full-time faculty member for the Information School at the University of Washington since 2015. My firm continues to publish research notes on risk, policy, privacy, and ethics through the "Reflections on Risk" series, of which there are five volumes. The research notes are written primarily by my students and remain relevant today to the questions they examine in detail. Through my monthly newsletter, "ASA News & Notes," I publish a column that usually connects several risk-related themes. Before the end of the year, I intend to be writing for a broader public audience. In the meantime, I am happy to return to an update of this book, since much of this advice is adaptable for both government institutions and private sector firms.

CHAPTER 1

AT HOME

We all want to be safe and secure at home, whether "home" is a house, an apartment, or a single room.

You have a right to think of it as your castle. Our homes are the places we start from and return to each day — the embodiment of our styles, the places into which we can both invite friends and retreat from the world. Whatever the circumstances, a home is a place where we want to feel safe. If we are lucky, our homes sit in neighborhoods where we feel part of communities.

Modern life presents us with a range of challenges, as our lives have become more complex. The lines between public and private life are increasingly blurred. We live not only in our homes but also in intricate social networks on the Internet.

Potential threats present themselves in many forms. Sometimes threats come from outside the home — robberies or break-ins — but as often the threat can come from something as simple as faulty wiring, a gas leak, or an exploding water heater.

Natural disasters — winter storms, floods, earthquakes, tornadoes, hurricanes — fall somewhere in between, causing us to rethink how long we can hold out without hot water or power or refrigeration. Though infrequent, natural disasters don't wait to happen until we have put a perfect personal emergency plan in place. You can take reasonable precautions at home that make unusual events less traumatic and less expensive as well. You might be familiar with some of these; others will be new. To have a plan and to be prepared is to know that you will be able to survive unfortunate events.

This chapter looks at how to think about what is reasonable where your home is concerned.

First, take all obvious precautions to reduce your safety risk.

Safety First
Burglaries are a common threat to homes and apartments alike. The Federal Bureau of Investigation estimates that a burglary happens every 15 seconds in this country.

What can be done to reasonably protect you from housebreakers? Most precautions are not very expensive. Do your doors lock? Are your windows secured? Do you know someone who lives near you who can keep a general eye out on your behalf ?

In the article "Cheap Home Security Tricks" on www.moneypit.com, windows are described as "the weakest link in home security." There's an easy fix from the hardware store for your windows for less than five dollars: Cut wooden dowels to fit inside the sash area of double-hung windows so that the windows cannot be opened from the outside far enough for someone to climb in. If you have casement windows, test the handles and locks to make sure they work and repair them if necessary.

Making sure that the locks on your windows and doors actually work is the first step. Learning to lock the windows and doors even when you are at home is the next step.

Like many of the issues involving personal risk that we will be looking at, there are two perspectives on "how safe is safe." Many homeowners prefer a security system that must be armed and disarmed as persons come and go. Discounts are frequently offered to homeowners by insurance companies if a security system is in place. But sometimes the logistics of security systems are frustrating for people with small children or the elderly. False alarms are also costly, so this is a decision that each family has to make for itself.

In the past few years, manufacturers have created home security products designed to streamline management of certain functions via an online connection. Many of these products are designed as do-it-yourself (DIY) installations. Amazon's products called Ring and Cloud Cam are two such wireless products, and you become the manager of the service that the products provide. (For more information on such online products, see Chapter IV)

While an argument can be made that putting a managed security service company's label near your front door warns off potential burglars, the other side of the argument is that such labels might advertise the fact that there really is valuable stuff inside. Seeing such labels, burglars may be confident that they can break in and get away before the security company or the police arrive.

You will want to ensure that all ground-floor windows lock and that basement or garage doors on the periphery are also locked. Do not leave ladders leaning up against your house to offer entry to the second story. Fence gates should be closed. Such reasonable precautions can mitigate a significant amount of risk, especially if practiced daily rather than only when you are on vacation.

Another measure you can take is to ensure that entry points such as the front and back door are well-lit, or that a motion detector is installed, with either a bright light or alarm that sounds when the home is approached in the dark. Consider illuminating your house numbers so that emergency responders can easily locate your home; reflective house numbers can be painted on the curb as well, which is where they will look first when responding to an emergency.

Risk Tips 1 & 2

Secure your home, then purchase an appropriate amount of homeowner's insurance.

Create a household inventory in case your home is damaged.

Gardens that are well-designed can also provide a degree of home security. Trees and bushes can be trimmed in such a way that it is difficult to move close to the house without being seen. Certain prickly bushes can be planted beneath windows that might otherwise appear to be easy to enter. Fences are frequently used to afford higher levels of privacy, but need to be paired with good outdoor lighting to be effective. Still another level of security can be offered by an observant dog.

You should also consider three other reasonably priced precautions for homes or apartments: fire extinguishers ($20-$40) for each floor of your house; a carbon-monoxide detector (about $20) to protect against gas leaks; and a roll-up rope ladder ($120-$150) to store near an upstairs window that would be the backup exit for your family in case of fire.

The final reasonable precaution to take when you move to a new home or apartment is to have the locks rekeyed. You have no way of knowing how many keys the previous homeowner may have distributed. Even though it is often easier to hand over a key to a service provider rather than be present at home when services are being performed, do be careful about whom you provide with keys to your home, even temporarily, since keys can be duplicated. The question "Who has keys to your home?" is one asked by most insurance appraisers as well as by officers when filling out a police report after a burglary. This same advice applies to a weekend cabin or vacation property, though you may wish to consider additional elements to secure it in your absence. In some parts of the country, this is common.

Special hurricane shutters, storm panels, impact-resistant windows or even garage-door-like coverings that roll down over large windows may be in order. It may also make sense to install a security system that is connected to an alarm company or to the police.

YOUR FOUR WALLS

For most people, their homes — whether apartments or homes that they rent or own — contain their most significant assets. In the years that we've been married, we've owned only three homes: one in the Midwest, one in up-state New York, and our current home in Seattle. Elements common to all three homes include the fact that each was an architecturally interesting older home with several stories, lovely windows and woodwork, hardwood floors, and front and back gardens.

We have lived in a 1918 house north of the University of Washington for more than 40 years. It sits in an urban neighborhood filled with trees and gardens, a neighborhood of families and friends. We renovated the house in 2005-2006, expanding a first-floor study and replacing the second story.

The work we did brought our house up to current standards and can serve as a checklist if you are planning to rent or purchase a home.

- Is the house secured to its foundation? (Our house was secured to the foundation for earthquake protection.)
- Does the house have a solid foundation? (New foot-

ings had to be poured to hold the weight of the renovated house.)

- Is the roof free of leaks and well-maintained? (The new roof was reinforced with hurricane clips.)
- Is the electrical service up to code? (All electrical components, including some knob-and-tube wiring, were replaced.)
- Is the heating system going to cost you an arm and a leg? (We removed the furnace and installed an energy-efficient heating system driven by a gas-fired boiler.)
- Are the windows and doors in good condition? (We added windows and replaced ones where the wood had deteriorated.)

Once the work was complete, we asked our insurance company for a reassessment of the value of our home, which triggered an increase in coverage on the structure.[3]

If you are purchasing a home, you may wish to make your offer contingent upon an examination and home inspection report on the home and the property on which it is sited to be sure both are up to code, and to identify any safety or security issues. To find an expert, check with your insurance company to see it has have recommendations, or check for online reviews in your city. Once you have the report, it is up to you to decide which recommendations to implement. Two things in particular to look for: 1) that the

---

3 For a more comprehensive list that also covers insurance issues, see Katherine Reynolds Lewis, "Protect Your Home (and Finances) from Disaster," *Money,* August 9, 2011, https://money.cnn.com/2011/08/09/real_estate/homeowners_insurance.moneymag/index.htm.

house has been tied down to the foundation, and 2) that the roof passes muster for high winds and/or tornadoes, depending upon where you live.

In the Northwest, earthquakes are the worst natural disasters to anticipate. Unfortunately, any house built before 1980 is not required by code to be tied down to its foundation. The engineering detail for the remedy was complex, especially when we were increasing the load on the foundation with two second-story dormers.

If it is possible, including such work as part of remodeling makes sense. The structure of the house can be modified by stages, once you have a clear picture of the larger risks that probably weren't considered when your home was built.

It took several months for the work of reinforcing the house and tying it down to the foundation to be completed. Deep holes had to be dug and reinforcing rods installed. Two pony walls on the house were opened from the outside and reinforced with rods and epoxy shafts driven down into the foundation. Heavy metal L-shaped braces were installed and drilled deep into the foundation as well.

We included these elements of reinforcement of our basement wall.

Extra security for the roof included hurricane hardware.

I acted as project manager for the renovation, and a large part of that work was behaving as a risk detective. We controlled the largest risk — that the project would fall behind or out of control — by living in the house's basement apartment for the duration. While that is often not possible or even imaginable, it is certainly worth thinking about remaining in the house to oversee smaller renovations.

I had remodeled the basement the year prior to the renovation, turning a darkroom into a small kitchen and my former office into a bedroom. An old utility bathroom was redone with laundry facilities. The 400-square-foot flat was completed by a living room that contained a couch and a chair, wall-to-wall bookcases, and a television set. There was one other risk independent of the work of the renovation: that my husband and I might get on each other's nerves being in such close quarters for twelve months. Adjoining the flat is my husband's garage, which he uses as a workshop, his bolt-hole, as it were. My escape was the garden.

INSURANCE

My husband and I lost the third story of our home in Rochester, New York, on a wintry evening three years before we moved to Seattle. A fire started from an elecrical short in the typewriter on which my husband was working. That floor of the house was my husband's study, and it contained the book manuscript he had been working on for several years, as well as thousands of books and other artifacts that were stored in the crawl spaces of the attic office behind the bookshelves — everything from camping equipment to our marriage certificate, childhood scrapbooks, and other family memorabilia.

Our post-fire work was featured in a front-page article in the *Rochester Community News* in 1974.

In a matter of moments, we lost a great deal that was not replaceable. On the positive side, no lives were lost and the firefighters were there almost immediately. In below-zero temperatures, they managed to cover and save count-less other books, artworks, and furniture on the first and second floors. Over the next week, friends and colleagues joined us to help try to identify frozen pages from mostly burned books that lay on our front lawn. We reconstructed an inventory of the library we had lost, to file as part of our insurance claim, which would allow us to rebuild that third story.

That leads directly to the issue of homeowner's insurance and why it's important to have a good policy, though the fire story probably has already clearly made the case. Oth-er types of disasters also can cause serious damage to your home. An insurance policy makes the difference between keeping your home and suffering an enormously expensive financial setback.

Nonetheless, depending upon where you live, it is difficult and expensive to get insurance riders to cover, for instance, floods or earthquakes or other types of natural disasters that might be common to that area of the country. We have seen just how devastating uninsured loss can be on the coastlines of New York and New Jersey from Hurricane Sandy; to that, we can add areas of the Gulf Coast that have not yet recovered from Hurricane Katrina.

Fortunately, most mortgage lenders require that homeown-er's insurance is carried to the value of the home loan they are making, and with a value set on your personal property inside the structures as well. You can research a number of reputable insurance companies.

The well-known ratings firm J.D. Power offers a site that compares the main companies. Renters can also purchase insurance from many of the same firms that covers the value of their personal property in a home or apartment.[4]

At the time of our fire, we did not have a good record of our possessions. Today, it's easy to use a digital camera to photograph each room of the house to create an inventory of cherished possessions. Websites and services such as Picasa, Dropbox, and Carbonite allow you to store such visual inventories on the internet as well as on a home computer. Home-inventory software programs can also back up to an off-site location.[5]

═══════════

Risk Tip 3

Ensure that your most valuable records are portable and stored in at least two different places.

═══════════

Had we photographed our bookshelves, it would have been easier to provide documentation to insurance investigators because we could have enlarged the photos and created a database by reading the titles on the spines of the books.

If you have other items of value, such as artwork, cameras, or jewelry, it is worth it not only to photograph them, but also to find the receipts for purchases and schedule them

4 "Ratings & Awards: Insurance," J.D. Power, accessed August 21, 2019, https://www.jdpower.com/business/ratings/industry/insurance.

5 Two of the more popular home-inventory software programs are Quicken's "Home Inventory Manager" and "DocuHome."

on your homeowner's policy by contacting your insurance agent. You can also buy a fireproof safe to keep the originals of vital documents, as well as tax returns and other materials. See the last section of this chapter to learn which vital home documents should be copied and stored off-site, so that you have access to them at all times.

I can read or remember the titles of my books from this photo.

ALERTS

You can request a range of alerts online that will bring text messages to your phone in the case of emergencies. Such alerts vary from bus-route or airline-tracking information to emergency alerts from schools, places of work, and government agencies. Be sure to set alerts to text you rather than send a voice message, in case cell service is overloaded during a disaster or emergency. Text messages are smaller in format than voice mails or emails and thus more likely to get through if some service is available.

For example, I have alerts set from the University of Washington, where I am a faculty member, which are mostly notifications of criminal incidents on or around the campus, but would also provide me directions in the event of a campus-wide emergency incident or a natural disaster. I have also signed up for Twitter feeds from the State of Washington Department of Transportation, so I have a feel for how traffic is flowing, and from Seattle's Metro bus service so that I know when service is delayed or rerouted. Another extremely useful Twitter feed comes from Seattle City Light, providing an outage map with estimated time to restoration of power.

I also subscribe to a Twitter feed that is actually a blog for the area where I live, and to another on Google Groups that covers a larger area in North Seattle. Both are a great way to find out about new businesses or get specific instructions in the case of an emergency. Seattle's Ravenna Blog proved especially useful during the Cafe Racer mass killings in 2012, as it linked to Seattle Police updates and provided additional updates on a shooter who had killed five people and was at large for hours. To find which alerts might be available in addition to any alerts that your employer might offer, try searching on your town or city's website.

It's also possible to invest in a personal mobile-alert service, which brings assistance for medical emergencies including falls, fire, invasion, or gas emergencies — and which works in and out of the home.[6]

---

6 One such system is Life Alert Mobile Service, (800) 360-0329.

Outdoors

Ideally, we'd all have a secure garage for our vehicles, but often cars or motorcycles are parked on the street and bicycles simply propped up near the home. It pays to have a security system on your car, to lock the car, and to park it near a street light. Bicycles should be locked up at home in the same way that they are locked up when ridden to other locations.

Look at other liabilities posed by common spaces outside your home, such as its sidewalks. While technically these are owned by the city, often tree roots or other displacements cause the sidewalk to become an unstable surface for walkers to use. Check city codes to see whose responsibility it is to maintain the sidewalks that are on your property.

Similarly, take time to clean out storm drains that sit on the street outside your home. Though this may not be your responsibility, damage that accrues from overflows during heavy rain or flooding usually occurs to your property, offering you a fine incentive to keep these drains open.

Cars and Bikes

A car can become a second home during a disaster. It's also a temporary home during unsafe weather conditions you may encounter while driving. I keep an extra pair of sturdy work boots in the trunk of my car, as well as an emergency pack[7] that contains drinking water, food bars, a reflective blanket, a lightweight poncho, a safety flare, tissues, a whistle, and an N-95 respirator mask. I also have extra fleece

---

7 I purchase emergency kits for home, office, and car from www. emprep.com. It is one of many sites that offer such supplies.

clothing, Gatorade, and energy bars, just in case I get stuck.

My "Evac Pack" in the trunk of my car, along with extras: water
bottle, tool kit, hiking boots, and extra wipes.

Gas tanks are kept at least half full at all times on our vehicles, in case gasoline would not be available during a disaster. It also pays to make sure your car radio works. In New York City during the 2003 power-grid outage, citizens used their car radios to bring news of what was happening. Residents of the New York and New Jersey coastlines used that same technique during Super Storm Sandy in October 2012.

Bicycles and motorcycles are good alternate modes of transportation when traffic is backed up, when gasoline is scarce, or when the terrain has been alerted during a disaster.

Neighbors
Another important component to home safety is your neighbors. I grew up in a small town where everyone knew

everyone else's name. My mother was part of a "community club" where women did everything from preparing emergency supplies for the town to discussing books they had recently read.

Even though most of us do not have the time in today's fast-paced world to take part in such activities on a regular basis, it makes sense to introduce yourself to those who live near you, and to provide mutually beneficial support.

We know our neighbors on all sides of our home. Two of them have keys to our house, just as we have keys to theirs. We let them know when we are planning to be away and ask them to keep an eye on the house. They know that means they should call the police if they see suspicious activity, and that they should call us if they note something unusual but not necessarily suspicious. We do the same for them when they vacation or travel. On a broader scale, our larger neighborhood has a blog that covers mostly crime-watch activity, referrals for contractors, neighborhood events and activities. Of late, we're working on an overall emergency plan for the neighborhood — and we're using the blog to alert neighbors on it.

Situational Awareness

Ours is an active neighborhood, with residents walking their dogs, or out for a walk or run. Many professionals exercise in early morning hours or in the evening when home from work. It's important to train yourself to become "situationally aware" when you are out by yourself in areas that are not well lighted or heavily trafficked. Use your eyes to "scan" the landscape for suspicious activity or persons. Always carry identification and a mobile phone. If you are listening to music, make sure that it is not so loud as to drown out sounds around you. A favorite trick of those who assault women in parks is to grab them from behind. Now that you know that, you can remain observant of those coming up behind you on a jogging or bike path. In the last chapter of this book, I discuss how to walk on the street when you are traveling. The same advice applies here: Do not look or walk with uncertainty. Walk confidently and report any problems that you have.

In the Neighborhood

Many cities have volunteer neighborhood organizations that take responsibility and become the communications liaisons with government agencies during a disaster. Seattle is a city that leads with its Seattle Neighborhoods Actively Prepare (SNAP) Program.

For the 312 households in the area where I live, we have formed a group to lead neighborhood disaster response. The 17 block captains are responsible for the families and homes they have volunteered to help in times of crisis. They have collected information on their residents, including how many people live in each home, and whether they have special needs or special skills that could be used during an emergency.

We have identified a home to act as a neighborhood meeting site, where block captains can report in, as well as homes to act as sites for first-aid and neighborhood care.

We have established leaders to be responsible for utility

control, search and rescue, disaster first aid, sheltering and special needs, communications, and damage assessment. Since 2011, the team has raised money to create emergency medical supply kits for each of the four zones covered, and has obtained more training in areas such as first aid and search and rescue. We will be prepared to maintain ourselves for three to five days at minimum. If your municipality does not have such a program, you can easily set one up by using materials on the websites of larger cities' emergency management operations. I recommend taking a look at the one created for Seattle, which has what is considered one of the most progressive emergency management offices in the country. This program can be replicated anywhere.

Emergency Preparations

For most of us, it is easier to buy extra batteries or maintain a spare tire for the car than it is to make an emergency plan and build an emergency kit. Issues or problems that are not right in front of us seem only remotely possible, and often do not seem worth planning for at all. As a risk specialist, I can assure you that I see this all the time, both in terms of personal and business safety.

Studies argue that we are hard-wired for optimism. In her book, *The Optimism Bias: A Tour of the Irrationally Positive Brain*, neuroscientist Tali Sharot discusses the tendency most of us have to assume that we will encounter positive events and underestimate the likelihood of negative events.[8] This certainly explains the behavior of senior executives and CEOs in large companies, and even many elect-

---

8 Tali Sharot, *The Optimism Bias: A Tour of the Irrationally Positive Brain* (New York: Pantheon Books, 2011).

ed officials — without their own confidence that the glass is usually half-full, they could not inspire their teams and drive successful levels of performance. But this bias toward optimism often leaves companies and families without emergency plans. Some businesses have plans, but many do not. An American Management Association study indicates that roughly 50 percent of businesses that have no emergency plan do not ever reopen for business after a major disaster.[9]

So you can see how an optimism bias can preclude making real preparations against potential emergencies or disasters, either at home or at work. If we cannot imagine a catastrophic event, it seems improbable. If it is improbable, it does not appear to merit serious attention. You would think there are enough examples in the world today to persuade anyone to make emergency preparations. Unfortunately, whether in business or at home, we find that the effort involved in thinking through what one would need to live off the grid for three to fourteen days is too depressing to get done, whether at work or at home.

I propose here to think about emergency preparations at home in the same way my company asks corporations to do it. We can best assess hazards where we live by using an x/y axis to describe the critical elements of *magnitude* (how severe?) and *frequency* (how often?).

An earthquake is a natural *hazard* of the West Coast, including the Pacific Northwest region; therefore, on my personal-risk chart, I want to look at how often they happen

9 Greg Livingston, *The Definitive Guide to Business Continuity Planning* (MIR3 Publications, 2011).

and how bad they are. In Florida, the natural hazard that would command this same sort of attention is a hurricane. In Oklahoma, natural hazards would include tornadoes and small earthquakes from fracking. In the Midwest, the key natural hazards would be flooding and tornadoes. In California, the natural hazards also include wildfires and drought — and more recently, several earthquakes of 6.0M or higher, with aftershocks that will continue for several months.

There are also *technological hazards*, such as nuclear power-plant leaks and major power outages, and *terrorist hazards* of explosions and biological and chemical threats.

You see how this part of threat analysis goes: When we apply the elements of magnitude and frequency, the results vary. In the Pacific Northwest, the frequency of major earthquakes is low but the magnitude is very high. In Florida, both the magnitude and frequency of hurricanes can be high. In the Midwest, the results can vary, so we would have to look across a range of years to rate this risk of flooding or tornadoes. In California, both the magnitude and frequency of wildfires is already high; and to that graph we can now revise the frequency of 6+M earthquakes in a particular region of the state.

So you should put together a personal plan that will stand you in good stead whether it's a smaller magnitude event — such as the loss of power for up to forty-eight hours — or a high-magnitude event like an earthquake or hurricane that could prevent city services from reaching you for an extended period of time. We know that many regular ser-

vices could become unavailable, including:
- Calling 911 for an ambulance.
- Reporting robberies or other losses to police or insurance companies.
- Retrieving cash from an ATM.
- Refilling a prescription.

The best way to think about what goes into an emergency kit is to assume that you will not have power or grocery or medical services during the disaster. Plan to be without services for three to five days, minimum; configure your emergency plan and your emergency kit accordingly. Store your emergency kit in a safe place in your home, checking at intervals to ensure that everything in the kit still works or is refreshed. At the same time, prepare your home so that sheltering there is not a burden to you or to your neighbors. Note that vegetarians or vegans will need to order special food kits.

═══════════════

Risk Tip 4

Create both an emergency management plan for your family to follow and an emergency kit that will allow you to live to off the grid for three to five days.

═══════════════

You can find more suggestions on a number of books and websites.[10] Remember that your list may need to include

---

10 The best website is FEMA's www.ready.gov/build-a-kit, with a parallel site for small businesses. One of the most exhaustive outlines of potential disasters and of additional measures that can be taken is to be found in Judith Kolberg's *Organize for Disaster* (Decatur, GA: Squall Press, 2004, 2005).

supplies that are particular to the region where you live or the types of disasters that occur there.

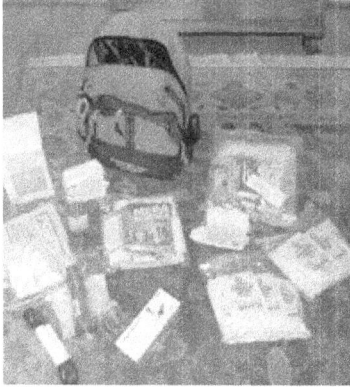

The contents of a backpack emergency kit; the front zippered pocket holds copies of vital home documents.

I keep our backpack in a main-floor hall closet that is midway between the front and back doors.

Because there's always the possibility that you will have to evacuate your home in case of major disaster, consider a portable emergency kit to grab and go.

For that same possibility, I also keep a nylon bag under my side of the bed that contains sturdy shoes as well as a set of clothing and a flashlight.

Flu

There's another type of risk that could keep you and your family at home for an extended period of time: a flu virus of one sort or another. Over the past 20 years, we've seen a variety of flu viruses spread in various countries. The simplest precaution you can take is to ensure that members of your family, especially older persons or pregnant women, have an annual flu shot. The vaccine's recipe is adjusted each year to fight the most current influenza strains.

The next most important step you can take is to stay home from work or school if you are sick. The flu spreads when persons in your environment sneeze or touch surfaces and leave the virus behind for you to pick up. Washing your hands frequently or using an alcohol-based hand cleaner cuts your risk significantly. If you can avoid touching your eyes, nose or mouth, you further cut that risk. (These days, when I get on an airplane or sit in any public space like a coffee shop, I use antibacterial wipes to eliminate what others have left behind on armrests, magazines, or table surfaces.)

Were any flu to turn into a pandemic flu, then I would also recommend staying away from public places and wearing a special particulate mask in the workplace or on an airplane.

Other precautions you might take for a pandemic event are included as part of general emergency plans and kits in the next section of this chapter.

Emergency Plans

In addition to your emergency kit, you should make an emergency plan that includes all your emergency phone contacts for your family and save it in a booklet as well as online. Other elements that should be part of your emergency plan:

- Identify a location where you will meet outside the neighborhood if your home is unavailable or if your neighborhood is on a police lockdown.
- Identify an out-of-state contact for everyone to notify with their safety status after an event.
- Identify where the shutoff valves are located in your home for gas, water, and electricity.
- Know how to evacuate your home in case of fire or gas leak — plan an escape route and practice the escape.
- Consider using a "Vial of Life," which contains all pertinent medical information for those living in your home. Place it on the front, upper right-hand shelf of your refrigerator, where emergency medical personnel know to look for it. You can purchase these vials in many drugstores at the prescription counter, or see details at www.vialoflife.com.

Your Emergency Kit[11]

Water: One gallon per person per day, three to fourteen days' worth

Food: Nonperishable, including food for special diets

First Aid Kit: One for home, one for car

Cash: In small bills, enough for three to five days

Tools:

- Eating utensils, including can opener and utility knife
- Battery-operated radio, extra batteries
- Flashlight(s), extra batteries
- Small sewing kit
- Compass and whistle
- Matches in waterproof container
- Wrench to shut off gas and water
- Work gloves
- One or more signal flares
- Rope ladder near second-story exit
- Plastic bucket
- Disinfectant, bleach, liquid detergent
- Battery-operated power tools such as drills, staple guns
- Portable camp stove and fuel
- One fire extinguisher per floor
- Toolkit with pliers, handsaw, duct tape, crowbar, sledgehammer

Clothing:

- Change of clothing and footwear
- Sturdy shoes or work boots

11 I double-checked my list against the City of Seattle's Office of Emergency Management brochure "Your Family Disaster Supplies Kit."

- Thermal underwear
- Rain gear
- Hat and gloves
- Blankets, sleeping bags

Special Items:
- Prescription medications and supplies
- Personal hygiene items
- Toilet paper
- Extra eyeglasses
- Baby supplies
- Garbage bags and ties
- Extra set of house and other keys
- Copies of or a spreadsheet listing insurance policies, credit cards, official identification, bank information
- Copies of other vital documents
- Pet food

Vital Home Documents

You should keep a collection of documents stored:
- In a waterproof container in your emergency kit
- Away from your home
- Off-site electronically

A homeowner's or renter's insurance policy is one key component. Imagine how quickly you will want to report any loss to your agent: What information do you need to store off-site or electronically so that you can do just that?

In addition to the policy and your agency's contact information, keep color copies of the documents in your wallet, including driver's license, credit cards, health insurance, and auto-insurance cards and passport.

You and your spouse or partner may also wish to consider whether you wish your executor to have passwords for various online accounts. Social media sites like Facebook now have protocols for providing access to notify friends and close or maintain accounts when the user dies. Other institutions with whom business is done electronically, like banks or insurance companies, may have more complicated protocols.

Other vital documents include your will and power of attorney, as well as your health-care-authority (Living Will) instructions. Your attorney might be able to pull up the documents, but not everyone knows who your attorney is, so it is easier to make sure also that your executor has copies of these documents.

Vital Home Documents

Home and auto policies

Passport

Driver's license

Credit cards

Immunization records

Other medical information, if relevant

Wills and medical directives

Bank-account numbers

Inventory list of investments

Household-goods inventory

Family records (birth and marriage licenses)

You should also have a concise list of beneficiaries of any life insurance or other financial annuities or investments where beneficiaries are named, and instructions on where to locate the titles to motor vehicles or other modes of transportation. This simplifies the job of the executor. What other documents might you need for yourself or your family in the midst of a high-impact event? The list shown above is a good place to start.

We tend not to want to think much about death. But in addition to making sure you have the vital home documents listed, you may wish to leave instructions about how you wish to die. For some, this is a simple outline of what steps you wish to be taken in the event your health fails, written to the person who will be in charge of your medical decisions. For others, it may be a set of instructions about whether you would like to have a funeral or a memorial service, along with any other details you'd like to plan. Most states now have nonprofit membership organizations that take the emotion out of funeral planning by allowing you to join and plan in advance of your death, so that your instructions can be followed in a straightforward manner. Planning for death makes it easier on those you leave behind and ensures that your wishes are respected.

Chapter II

At School

I grew up in a small town where everyone knew my sister and me. We were well cared for from our earliest days, even though my mother worked part time. Despite having a vivid imagination, I can't remember any sense of danger or menace. Though I chaffed at times at the lack of privacy, I know just how lucky we were to have been raised in such a town and time, where everyone knew you and little went unreported to your parents.

Today, television, smartphones, and social media sites make us far more aware of how others outside our family or community might behave — as well as threats that can face children in different parts of the country. We know that children can be mistreated or hurt no matter where they live. We want our children to remain children as long as possible, but also to be aware of the potential threats they can face as they grow up.

After the mass shootings of children in Newtown, Connecticut in December of 2012, I have modified the early part of this chapter. I am not a psychiatrist, nor am I a police officer. I do not want to sound prescriptive, nor do I want to make you feel paranoid. This chapter is divided into sections that cover the growth of a child from earliest days to risks that a new college student might want to think about. At the heart of the chapter is the question of how to manage risk, first for your child and then how to teach your child to manage their own risk.

What I do know is a function of being around children since my early work as a lifeguard, and from also being a parent. Sometimes I was aware of the risks that children face, but there were times when I ignored or accepted the risk that was present in the situation. Based upon their own values, parents need to make determinations about what is an acceptable level of risk for their children until it is time to turn the decision-making over to the child.

Day Care or Pre-school

If you are like many parents, you will be looking for a trust-worthy caregiver to take care of your child when you are working. How do you find such a person or facility? Some are lucky enough to work for large companies that provide an on-site day care service where you can visit your child during the day. But most of us find caregivers through word of mouth or by careful research. What should you be looking for?

Risk Tip 5

Do your own homework on care providers.
Obtain references and check them out.

Double-Check

Just like you would check references when you hire an employee at work, you should follow a similar procedure at home. Whether you are considering an individual caregiver or a facility, ask for three references. Double-check your state's health and human services department to see if there are known outstanding violations by the caregiver. Visit the location and inspect it for cleanliness. Once you've been there, an unscheduled drop-in visit to ask a follow-up question will allow you to compare the look of the place when cleaned up for potential clients and during a regular day.

I would say that the references requirement should apply also to anyone you are considering as a babysitter for your child, especially for a baby. Many schools now offer courses in babysitting for which a student can obtain a certificate. Organizations like the American Red Cross offer first aid courses for babysitters. You want to be sure that the babysitter, whether through training or experience, knows how to change diapers, feed, and calm a crying child. The sitter should also know basic first aid and how to call you or 911, if necessary. I always left a set of written instructions for babysitters that included a basic introduction to my child and his habits as well as bedtimes, activities of interest, and which foods in the refrigerator the sitter was welcome to eat.

Once your child is old enough, she/he will be able to give you feedback on the caregiver. Until that time, it's your responsibility to ensure that you have left your child in a safe place with an attentive caregiver.

Values Alignment

Despite all the background checks you do, sometimes there's not a good way to find out about whether or not your values and those practiced at the school match up. Pre-school represents a child's earliest opportunity to use manners, values, and behaviors learned at home. Here, too, you will want to be concerned with the child's safety and happiness. If your child's behavior at home changes markedly once in pre-school, it's appropriate for you to spend time with their teacher(s) and/or in the classroom as a helper to see what the cause might be. This is also a time to observe without judgment (if such a thing is possible) whether your child is making friends at school or in the neighborhood. If not, how can you help without becoming another source of pressure for the child? You also want to make sure that your child is not behaving as a bully, or being bullied.

═══════════

Risk Tip 6

Does the school you are looking at have a special focus? Can you speak with the teachers and form a preliminary opinion about fit?

═══════════

Primary School

Parents agonize over the selection of their child's first real school. Sometimes they even move the family to an area so that they might qualify to have first preference at a school in the neighborhood. But, especially at this age, the heart of teaching is still by example and by discussion in the home.

My stepdaughters spent summers with us from the time they were six and three years old. That first summer, my husband said to me that kids go by what they experience, not by what people tell them. I think that's an important lesson for all parents to remember, as children are able to spot hypocrisy at an early age. Because they spent the bulk of the year away from us, we wanted them to be self-starters, to think things through before they made decisions. By the time they were in high school, they were making most of their own decisions, at least in the summer months. As long as they had thought carefully about the pros and the cons of an issue, we let them make the decision. I believe they applied this approach to the choices they made about where they would go to college as well; and that they continue this practice with their own children today. When our son came along, he was raised with the same approach, building a strong foundation for independent but considered decision-making that has stood him in good stead as well.

Your child's circle of influence gets much larger once she/he is in primary school. You'll start to hear about kids and teachers you may not know, and there will be requests to spend time at other kids' homes. You'll want to meet the kids and at least one of the parents before saying yes — perhaps dropping off and picking up your child to get some better sense of the other family.

When he heard I was writing this chapter, a friend recommended a website, *parentmap.com*, that has an article titled "Five Easy Questions: What You Should Ask Before the Sleepover."[12] Here are the questions from the article: "Is there a gun in your home? Who's watching the kids? Is someone monitoring the Internet? Will the kids be going out or staying in? Is there anyone else in the house?"

Though I've been urging you to be alert from the moment you first entrust your child with someone else, here is where that principle begins to be applied consistently. Is your child happy in school? If you see signs that your child has become withdrawn, secretive, or aggressive, perhaps it's time to have a discussion with their teacher to be sure that there is no bullying going on, to or by your child. Are there problems on the playground during recess that the teacher might not be aware of? Work to gain your child's confidence over any problems or issues, but do also ask the teacher to help you identify the cause of your child's unhappiness. Parents have a big investment in children feeling safe and confident at school from the outset, so that the idea of school does not become painful to a child early in life.

You'll need to teach your child about strangers and about how to get help if you are not there. Most schools will also drill children on what to do in case of fire or outside threats. In such matters, wherever you can, do reinforce those public safety lessons. If your child carries a phone, teach them the difference between the times when they would call 911 and when they would call you first.

12 Linda Morgan, "Five Easy Questions: What You Should Ask Before the Sleepover," *ParentMap*, September 26, 2012, https://www. parentmap.com/article/five-easy-questions-what-you-should-ask-be-fore-the-sleepover.

Most of all, here and at all other times in your child's life, model the manners and behaviors you expect. If you are rude to others, chances are high that your child will be rude. If you shout, scream, or whine at your spouse, expect to see the same unpleasant tactics from your child. If you talk about people behind their back, don't be surprised when your child sounds mean when describing some other child. You are your child's first teacher of what is right or wrong, of what is appropriate or inappropriate. And you are responsible for your child's behavior, especially at this age.

MIDDLE SCHOOL AND HIGH SCHOOL

Middle school can be tough for all but the most popular members of a class. Kids start to think with their hormones. Risky examples of behavior seem to abound. The primary school is usually smaller than the middle school, so there is a whole new element of complexity to consider where possible influences are concerned. It's at this age that young girls often give up sports and interest in science and math, choosing instead to be seen as attractive to boys who are far more immature than they. One would hope that your largest challenge would be ensuring that homework is done and turned in. On the other hand, here's where a child's interests in sports or the arts can begin to flourish.

My son, James, took up the trombone in primary school, but it was not until he got to Eckstein Middle School in Seattle that this interest took real shape. He was lucky enough to join the band program, led by Cuautehmoc "Moc" Escobedo, affectionately called "Mr. E." by his musicians. He ended up in the jazz band on the bass trombone. Music took time every day after school. Moc recommended a fine trombone teacher for him to take private lessons. James loved the discipline of playing music as part of a group, and in particular the jazz notion of improvisation. Early on, James recruited me to help support the band program by building a strong parent support group. Eventually, the parents' group ended up recording all the bands at Eckstein and producing an annual CD that raised money to support purchases of equipment for the band program. Some parents went to baseball games to watch their sons play. We went to jazz concerts and competitions, sharing that interest in jazz and improvisation all the way through high school. Interestingly enough, both Moc in middle school and Scott Brown at Roosevelt High School were themselves trombone players. They set the standard. In a *Seattle Times* article, Scott Brown, the Roosevelt jazz band director, made an astute set of observations about the rewards of being a player: "You are establishing values ... of team work, of personal expression, having your own voice, but be willing also to listen to what others have to say...most of these kids are not going to go on to be professional musicians. But whatever career path they choose, this is going to be good for them....they develop a strong sense of self, and the ability to respond under pressure and be in front of people with poise."[13]

For our family, James' first jazz teacher, Moc Escobedo set the standard, as a teacher with passion, ethics, and an astounding ability to listen to students and to earn their trust.

---

[13] Lynne K. Varner, "Seattle-Area Schools Score Big at Essentially Ellington," Opinion Northwest, *Seattle Times*, May 13, 2013, http://blogs.seattletimes.com/opinionnw/2013/05/13/seattle-area-schools-score-big-at-essentially-ellington/.

James learned discipline, teamwork, and the criteria at stake when the band competed against others in the Northwest. With such outside interests in sports or performing arts, it's easier to avoid some forms of reckless behavior.

Risk Tip 7

If your child is considering a sports team or jazz band or theater group, can you perform a version of a reference check on the person who will coach them? Given the cases of coaching abuse in the news, this seems especially important.

Technology Risks

Middle school is about the age that children get smartphones and their own personal computers. Perhaps parents believe that it is easier to keep track of their child by calling or texting. While that may be true, a smartphone is not a babysitter; rather, it is a powerful tool for the child to disappear into, spending more time texting or posting photos or Facebook updates than doing homework or interacting face to face. Social media sites like Facebook can disrupt attention spans, provoke unhealthy popularity contests, or even cause students with poor self-images who are bullied to commit suicide. (See Chapter IV on social media effects.)

What can you do? Before gifting the device to your child, have a frank chat about how data never really disappears from the internet even though you delete it. Explain that the minute you set up such a site, you need to be thoughtful and judicious in setting up your privacy settings, in the choice of "friends," and on the types of posts or status updates that might constitute TMD ("too much data"). Set guidelines around use of the device. Finally, remind your child that photos and posts on sites like Facebook and Twitter can be used as evidence in court cases.

Health Risks

The most common health risks at this age come from alcohol, drugs, and sex, as the young person tries hard to fit in. Ask your child about their school day. Be involved in their lives. The closer you are, the easier you can identify issues away from home. Try to provide a safe listening environment. Look for physical and emotional warning signs: bruises, marks, scratches. Help with homework. Attend school events such as plays, concerts, and sporting events. If your home is one where kids feel comfortable gathering, be sure that you're present, and that your own rules are clear. Don't leave kids alone at home when they have friends over, whether you trust them or not. Often it won't be your child who misbehaves, but rather someone who drops in.

This is also a great age to encourage your child to become a volunteer. Many schools have programs where your child can tutor another child. Or perhaps your child can join you in volunteer activities you undertake. It is never too early to set the habit of giving back.

Bullying

There is no shortage of bullies in the world. It's difficult to explain to a scared child that their bully probably has self-esteem issues that lead to belittling or hurting others when what the victim experiences is anger or sarcasm or something even worse. Reporting bullies is never easy for a child, and it may be that you will have to step in and speak with school authorities. If your child is small or petite, you may wish to consider martial arts training, which may also increase children's self-confidence.

Drugs/Alcohol

Schools will spend a certain amount of time discussing drugs, guns, and alcohol, with programs such as DARE (Drug Abuse Resistance Education), but here is an important area for parents to also weigh in on. Just as your personal values may dictate whether or not you want your child to learn a martial art, you'll want to align discussions of peer pressure with other values-based discussions you've had with your children as they grow.

There were many times when my parents said no to a request I was making — as I got older, almost always the response was based in the belief that "we don't do things just because others do them. We stop and think, then make our own decisions."

Commuting

There are many ways to get to middle or high school. Parents often drop off and pick up their kids. If the school is close enough, kids walk with their friends. Buses are also a means of transport as early as primary school. Remind your child to remain alert and polite at the bus stop rather than zoned out on electronic devices.

Though riding on a bus may seem like an ideal situation to show high spirits and to act out, it's important to explain to your child that the bus driver is in charge. The driver is also the person to whom you report any suspicious behavior that harms yourself or other riders.

RISK TIP 8

If your child has never ridden on public transit make this an experience the two of you can share, so your child gets a look at the bus environment with you along the first time.

EMERGENCY PREPAREDNESS

No matter what level of education your child is at, the school should be conducting training and drills so that students know what actions to take in an event of a fire, lockdown, or earthquake. Calmly reinforce the school's training by providing a context in which, as a child grows older, they understand public safety issues and how to respond without anxiety: Where are the exits to a building? What is the safe place to which you and your classmates go when evacuated? Why is it important to follow the directions of the person in charge?

If you as a parent take such drills seriously, so will your children. You have only to remember real school emergencies to know how important such training is. Let your child bring home the lessons learned at school and teach you.

Risk Tip 9

Reread the discussion on how to create an emergency plan for your family that is in Chapter I. Then be sure your child knows how to reach you or where to meet you if it is not possible to meet at home.

After-School Activities

It's not unusual for kids to be caught up in after-school practice sessions for sports or performing arts events until nearly dinnertime. Make it a practice for the family to know where the child is. Buses can sometimes be used by transients, drug addicts, or drunks, or travel through crime-prone neighborhoods, so if there is no one at home when they arrive, ask the child to call you to let you know when they are home. Though it is not always possible, the safest way for your kids to travel is in pairs, whether walking or on a bus.

General Physical Safety

Some of the matters I touch on lightly in this chapter, such as work, technology and travel, are covered in greater depth in subsequent chapters. Physical safety is an ongoing theme. Teach your child to be aware of their environments and situations. Also, teach them to think these situations through by walking them through the questions involved.

In general, know where your child is, especially after school and in the evenings. Set a policy for checking in and for curfews so that there is not any room for misunderstanding. This is the age where your job is really to balance the need to give the child progressively more independence but keep them out of trouble, whether in school or with the law.

Finally, if your child is assaulted, make sure that the authorities are notified. It is extremely difficult to improve public safety if the data is not there to support where and when problems occur.

COLLEGE

From the time I was a small child, I wanted to move to a big city and attend the University of Iowa. It was and is an awesome research university with an international population of students. My parents understood my ambition to go to college and complimented me for earning money to do so. In high school, I took the "college prep" curriculum. As "Mr. E." was to my son, James, so too was Loren Larson for me: Mr. Larson taught me how to read literature, write well, and think at a high level. He taught voice and band as well. Though I will never be a great musician, I learned to love music; and I played a coronet and sang in a girls' sextet. I worked from the time I was twelve years old, through high school, at many types of jobs to save money. I received a modest scholarship for my freshman year at the university, and then worked my way through undergraduate and graduate degrees.

Some parents choose to put them in private schools for K-12 education, wanting their child to be well-prepared for an outstanding college placement and to avoid the challenges that may come from an uneven public school education. One of the greatest barriers to college degrees today is the astounding cost of that education. It's not too early to begin thinking about how the costs will be managed, especially if you have more than one child to educate. How much of that cost will you absorb, and how much of that education do you plan to have your child accomplish through student loans? Will your child work their way through school? Will your child leave home to attend college? Where is the best fit for your child in today's educational system?

Risk Tip 10

When your children are born, make a strategic plan for how your family will handle the expense of college.

It is at this point in the chapter that I leave off addressing the questions to parents, and begin to address the student directly. For this section of the chapter, I am fortunate to have the recommendations of Emily Oxenford Hayes and Devin Luco, former ASA interns who shouldered their own way through undergraduate degrees, and then did their graduate level work at the University of Washington's Information School.

Behavioral Choices

For many, college is the first time that students make decisions away from their parents' eyes. Though they could also have skulked about in high school, here they are truly on their own — they can choose to skip classes, party too hard, or form problematic associations, or even become overly isolated, depressed, and reclusive. The behavioral choices are their own.

―――――――

Risk Tip 11

Ensure that your children are making decisions on their own, with your guidance, from an early age. If they already make independent decisions, they have precedent for how to handle new challenges in college.

―――――――

Alerts

The 2007 mass shootings of students at Virginia Tech were a wakeup call to institutions of higher learning. Whether you live on campus or not, take advantage of the mass notification systems that most colleges now have in place. Such systems are aligned with campus police and emergency response teams, to provide text message alerts on matters of public safety, including buildings that are shut down for various reasons. If you commute to the campus, you may also want to turn on alerts from your local transit provider, so that you are made aware of delays or road closures.

Be aware of your surroundings, whether you are on or off campus. Walk purposefully in well-lighted areas and with others whenever possible. If you are threatened, robbed, or assaulted, be sure to report it to authorities.

Electronic Devices

Ensure that you have serial numbers and descriptions of your electronic devices stored somewhere away from those devices. Be smart about how you use the devices. Of all the alerts I have received from the University of Washington

Police in the past several years, most are about robberies of smartphones taken from owners at public locations such as bus stops. As I indicate in the fifth chapter of this book, when traveling (in this country or internationally), I try to keep such devices out of public sight for just this reason. I never wear earphones in public situations either, because I want to be able to use my eyes and ears to stay safe.

Plagiarism

No longer is a parent available to read and edit your papers, or to discuss performance with the teacher. Work done in college is at another level entirely, and there is no third person in the relationship between you and your instructor. The largest personal risk in the work that you do in college can be avoided by always providing proper citations and references to where your ideas come from. In theory, all students are taught how to footnote in middle or high school, so this should not be an issue. In its code of conduct statement on academic integrity, here is what the University of Washington has to say to students:

> *"The essence of academic life revolves around respect not only for the ideas of others, but also their rights to those ideas and their promulgation. It is therefore essential that all of us engaged in the life of the mind take the utmost care that the ideas and expressions of ideas of other people always be appropriately handled, and, where necessary, cited. For writing assignments, when ideas or materials of others are used, they must be cited. The format is not that important—as long as the source material can be located and the citation verified, it's OK. What is important is that the material be cited. In any situation, if you have*

a question, please feel free to ask. Such attention to ideas and acknowledgment of their sources is central not only to academic life, but life in general."[14]

In college, you may be asked in some of your courses to take home examinations and/or to complete group assignments rather than individual ones. You will have a number of factors to balance in such situations. If it is a group assignment, then you will need to work hard as part of the group to minimize the impact someone else's neglect/shoddy work can have on you. If it is a take-home examination, then do the work yourself, for yourself. Again, in theory you will have been taught about the penalties for cheating in middle and high school. Add what you learned there to the story of the undergraduate cheating scandal at Harvard University in 2012, where roughly half of the undergraduate students in a course received a "required to withdraw" ruling.[15]

If you wish to earn a degree, then earn it with your own hard work.

If you do poorly on an exam or paper, do sit down with your instructor to ask for additional guidance. Nearly every

---

14 University of Washington (UW) Statement on Academic Integrity. This statement is taken directly off my course website for the operational risk courses I teach to graduate students, and is part of the "boilerplate" language used on most UW course websites. For additional guidance, see the full explication at https://www.washington.edu/cssc/for-students/academic-misconduct/.

15 Galen Moore, "Harvard Stops Short of Expulsion in Cheating Scandal Verdict," *Boston Business Journal,* February 1, 2013, https://www.bizjournals.com/boston/blog/mass_roundup/2013/02/harvard-cheating-scandal-verdicts.html.

college has a writing center or other services to help with homework, as well as academic advisors who can also be of assistance.

════════════════

Risk Tip 12

The habits that you form in college will remain with you most of your life. Be conscious and modify habits that do not lead to success.

════════════════

Assignments and Deliverables

Please take a look at the fourth chapter of this book and apply the technology lessons to your college work. In particular, save your files often while you are working on them. Back up your work to an external device, or invest in continuous online backup. Invest in applications recommended by your college, usually available at reduced prices through special licensing agreements.

It should not probably need to be said, but do not use your college network for illegal downloading. Malware exists on many peer-to-peer file sharing programs. Though other students may be doing it and not getting caught, know that most colleges monitor their networks for such behavior.

Planning Your Future

Find an advisor or a faculty mentor who can help guide you, once you know what you are aiming for in terms of a major. Consider opportunities for networking events or professional associations, where you can interact with those already working in the field of interest. Find out if your college has set up internship programs from which you might benefit, both in terms of experience and an accomplishment on your resume.

By the time you are ready for an internship or a full-time job, you will have developed your own personal brand. Make sure that your LinkedIn profile aligns with your social media posts, that it looks and sounds professional and that there are no posts that would cause recruiters not to consider you for a position. If you add faculty members to Facebook, make sure that your page is professional. Be mindful of postings to be sure they pass the sniff test where a potential employer could be concerned.

FINAL THOUGHTS HERE

With your guidance, your child can love attending school, encountering new ideas and becoming part of an institution larger than herself or himself. College should be a magical time in one's life, where you learn how much you do not already know; and spend more time thinking, reading, and writing — making connections from books and ideas.

I prefer to think of college as a time where you truly grow into yourself rather than as the ticket you must punch to find a good job. Managing your personal risks in college is part of growing into yourself.

Many undergraduates and certainly most of my graduate students are holding down a full-time job as they work on their degrees. The next chapter is for them, and for those who are just beginning to look for a job in the marketplace.

CHAPTER III

AT WORK

For my first job as a lifeguard and one that followed at the psychiatric hospital, I was an employee and had to learn both the culture of the job and how to get along with my fellow workers. I had increasing levels of responsibility in all my jobs, and I realize only now how much I benefited from working from such an early age, and from being exposed to so many different types of work environments, many of them dysfunctional.

When I became an executive responsible at times for several hundred people, my perspective was refined by the experience of leading others. Contrary to what some might think, there is no magic manual to read or course to attend that will teach enough about how to lead large numbers of people to work on behalf of the company's mission.

Whether at a small business or a large corporation, I found that my colleagues did enjoy setting a high bar and being the best at what they did. They were proud that their work made a difference.

We spend a good deal of our waking hours working, usually 40 hours a week or more. Though old patterns are starting to change, and some workers utilize technology to work from remote locations, most Americans still spend most of that time in the office Mondays through Fridays. It's often more time than we spend awake at home with our families and friends.

Some people work more than one job to make ends meet. Others are pursuing college degrees to increase their chances of advancement at work. Still others may be caring for an aging parent while trying to balance the responsibilities of parenthood. There are many reasons that those 40 hours at work can turn out to be a pressure cooker and lead to a higher level of risk for everyone in the workplace, especially in a tough economic climate.

When you mix persons from different environments, each of whom has a different set of personal challenges, it's a wonder that work actually works most of the time. It's my own experience that it works best when employees share a common purpose that is larger than any one of their lives. When employees are proud of their place of work, when they strive to make sure that the company delivers on its mission, then that common purpose often transcends job titles.

Most of the risk in the workplace comes from situations in which people — managers or colleagues — act thoughtlessly, exhibiting behaviors that are threatening or frightening to others.

You can start at the beginning of the employment cycle to investigate whether you can find out what you are getting into, and to make plans and take reasonable precautions. If you are in a situation where you already are feeling trapped, please read on. There may be thoughtful actions that you can take that will benefit both your situation and the workplace in general.

RESEARCHING THE COMPANY

Think of yourself as a risk detective when you start your job search. It's worth it to learn everything you can about the culture of a company before you begin work there. Of particular interest is the company's mission and values. Are they aligned with the work you are interested in doing, and does the mission align with your own values? Find whatever you can to familiarize yourself with both, and remember that those public statements do count for something. Look at annual reports and media profiles. Check any references you can find to the company via an internet search. Are there negative articles about turnover at the top, or about "cleaning house," or stories about customers' privacy not being protected?

When you go into a job interview, there usually is a point where you are asked if you have any questions. You may wish to pick and choose among the questions below, based upon the research you have already done:

- Does the company have a values statement or a code of conduct?
- If it's a publicly traded company, then you can search online for the firm's "10K filing" with the Securities and Exchange Commission and look in the section titled "Risks."
- Is there a human resources (HR) department?
- If it's a smaller company, how are HR issues handled?
- Is this a new position? If not new, then why did the last person leave?
- If you are being hired to solve a problem, ask for as much detail as possible about that problem.

If you have this information, you'll be able to make a deliberate decision about whether working in that situation could be a real opportunity for growth.

Making Your Mark

If you get the job, you will want work to ensure that your performance is above average in assignments that you are given. If you deliver on time and within budget for your boss, you are entitled to find ways to ask for increasingly more complex assignments.

If you have difficulty completing an assignment, be sure to talk with your boss before the deadline overtakes you. A deadline has its share of risks for both of you. It may be that you simply need some restatement of the goals or a better understanding of the importance of the assignment. Believe me that most managers will appreciate being approached before the deadline is compromised. Finally, volunteer for projects that you can see will stretch the talents you are already exercising on behalf of the company, especially if such projects will put you in touch with other parts of the company. In a book with almost the same name, Sheryl Sandberg calls this "leaning in."

On the Job

Despite our best efforts at finding a good place to work, problems can sometimes arise through no fault of our own. It may be a new employee who develops a set of problems that follow him/her into the workplace. Or it may be an external event that resonates through a whole city. Whatever the type of risk, it's worth thinking through what actions you can take to lessen the risk.

═══════════

Risk Tip 13

After you do the informal research, report suspicious or inappropriate behavior at work. Document in your own words both the incident and and the date you reported it

═══════════

If you are alert to changes in the workplace that create stress and anger, you will have mastered the most effective precaution.

Large companies have human resources departments that protect employees' rights and privileges. Many large companies also have hotlines or other programs where employees can report suspicious or problematic behavior by managers or other employees. Your rights are generally well-protected in such a corporate environment.

Smaller companies cannot always afford an HR manager. The closest approximation would be either a general manager or the CEO. If the company is still growing, with just a few employees, you often are working in close quarters, usually with more than enough work on your plate. Unless the owner of the small company has created an employee handbook that spells out expectations and guidelines around professional behavior, you will have to sit down with them to discuss your concerns directly. Try to frame the conversation in such a way that you are not just complaining, but perhaps offering to help put together an employee handbook to clarify expectations around such items as expected dress, hours of work, treating fellow employees and customers with respect, and even an emergency management plan for the small business.

Reporting suspicious behavior can be fraught with challenges. The established reporting structures at work may be informal or based upon seniority, and it may not be clear to whom you would report problems; it pays to observe how things work before you jump in. There may not be the regard for due process or confidentiality that a professional HR manager brings to the situation in a larger company. And, just as in large corporations, managers or employees may face harassment issues of several types.

Unfortunately, many problems still go unreported in the workplace because of a fear that the person will not be believed, especially when the issue is one between a manager (power) and an employee (no power). Some managers get away with intimidating their employees on a daily basis for years because they are never reported. While the aim of employee-rights programs is to do what is right, and while the majority of such programs, including whistle-blower programs, do work, reporting suspicious behavior can negatively mark the employee who files the report and may compromise future job growth. Before you act, the only way to find out how those who report things are treated is to closely observe the workplace you are in. Then you can decide how to present your concerns. I want to summarize everything I have said another way, especially in light of excellent books like Sheryl Sandberg's *Lean In*.[16]

At some point in your career, you may find yourself reporting to a manager whose personal skills leave something to be desired. In such situations, it's important to ensure that you understand your assignments and your manager's assessment of your performance. There is a fine line between being respectful and an active listener. You must ask enough questions to complete the work appropriately. Part of your job is in fact to get along with your manager. In an active work environment, it's inevitable that you will hear remarks about your manager. If others seem to be having the same challenges as you, then it's worth talking with the human resources department to see if there is guidance it might offer. This applies all year round, not just when you have received a performance review or critique of your work on a specific project.

If you are identified as being on a leadership track, then usually you will be able to select a mentor from some other part of the company. A mentor can be especially helpful in understanding whether or not your own development

16 Sheryl Sandberg, *Lean In: Women, Work and the Will to Lead*, (New York: Knopf, 2013).

needs fine tuning. A mentor is not a person to whom you bring problems or complaints about your boss, but rather a senior leader with significant experience who can discuss other tools you might use to grow in your current role, and who can help you identify your next role.

Harassment

Bullying or harassment based upon hierarchy is a particularly troubling behavior to report unless an employee can provide witnesses because the victim is afraid that they will not be believed. The best strategy is to try never to be caught alone with a bully and to document and report situations where others have observed the bullying. The behavior may disappear if the situation is handled professionally. In this and in each other situation described here, it is best to keep a record of dates, incidents and the reporting that you did. If you can find no recourse within your company, you may wish to file a complaint outside the company.

Employees, especially women, sometimes feel that reporting sexual harassment marks them in the eyes of management, whether in a large company or a small business. Concerned that they will not be believed, they try to ignore or handle such harassment on their own. This is as true for men who are sexually harassed as it is for women. Utilize the same strategies as I suggested for a bully: Try not to be caught alone with the harasser and keep your own records on who else might have witnessed the behavior. Unfortunately, if the culture permits such behavior, no matter the size of the company, the possible outcomes seem to be either moving to another part of the company, entering into a coerced relationship where the one who holds power is in charge of both the relationship and future employment, or leaving the job. Assuming that you are an intelligent and alert team player, what can you do to minimize the possibility of workplace bullying or sexual harassment? The key here, in companies large and small, is to let management know. This is best accomplished by asking for a private appointment and making as clear a report as possible of basis of your concerns, providing examples of the behavior to which you object.

If you are an observer of instances of bullying or harassment, or if you hear someone threatening another employee, consider offering to stand witness for the victim if they decide to report it to HR.

Report such behavior yourself when you see suspicious behavior, whether it is happening to you or to a member of your team. If employees are unable to resolve a pattern of harassment on their own, they should consider the following in this order, depending on the management structure of the company:

- **First**: Review the company's personnel handbook for any defined process for redress of such claims.
- **Second**: Contact the HR representative or, if applicable, the union representative.
- **Third**: Contact your supervisor, or, if applicable, your supervisor's supervisor, or the owner or a company officer (CEO, president, vice president).
- **Fourth**: If the above are ineffective or inapplicable, consider retaining an employment-law attorney for advice and assistance.

Notwithstanding the steps above, if an employee determines that the culture of the company is such that harassment is not discouraged or addressed in a positive manner, it may be time to find a new employer.

Social media amplified sexual harassment charges against powerful corporate executives in 2017 when the phrase #MeToo was popularized. From the stories that have emerged across every type of workplace, I feel obliged to offer some additional advice to women or men who work:

- With strangers, handshakes with a stiff elbow reduce the likelihood of being pawed.
- Do not agree to meet with an agent, a recruiter or a hiring manager in a hotel room. Find a public place.
- Resist all offers to have a drink after work with your manager unless the whole team is participating.
- Find ways to avoid delivering materials to your boss outside the office.
- Meet for lunch with your boss only in public places.
- Arrive late and leave early from holiday parties.
- If you are verbally harassed or excluded from work assignments as a result of following this advice, report it further. The workplace is far more sensitive to such reports these days.

VIOLENCE

Although you may be reluctant to report bullying or harassment, the highest-risk behaviors deserve prompt and clear reporting to management because they threaten everyone in the workplace. A sudden and sometimes violent change in behavior in an employee can be frightening to observe. Such altered behavior is hard on everyone in the workplace, even if it may not be life-threatening. Of course the reasons vary. It could be from personal trauma such as a pending divorce, life-threatening illness, or strained financial condition. In any of these cases, the person feels like their back is up against the wall and that they are without resources. Or perhaps the person has had a poor performance review, which they view as unfair and untrue. Each of these types of situations have, in some cases, led to active shooter workplace violence.

It's the job of the manager to try to speak with the person, who is probably not able to see that their behavior is affecting the workplace for everyone else in the environment.

If a manager is not detecting the behavior, check your own observations with others on the team, and then make sure that your manager understands that it is behavior that is problematic to the team.

Here are some behaviors that may be early warning signs of the potential for violence:

- Reclusive and/or aggressive behavior
- Anger over small things
- Excessive complaints
- Overreactions to problems
- Making threats
- Erratic attendance
- Disruptive behavior in meetings

As a manager, I listened to employees who displayed one or

more forms of the behavior described above. With few exceptions, I felt it best that they first try to manage their situations, and I offered them paid time off to get themselves back on track. In other cases, there were medical or other challenges in the family, and it turned out that I could find them community services available by a simple referral. Often the most important thing I did was to simply listen, which was a form of active support.

If the situation looked as though it was the result of more than exhaustion and anger, then it was reported to HR. It is entirely possible for an HR manager to arrange for counseling, anger management training, or other assistance such as a leave of absence for a troubled employee. Given a company's investment in training skilled workers, taking the time to try to fix the problem makes the most sense — unless the behavior is so outrageous that it threatens others in the workplace, in which case the HR department may in some cases file a police report and/or terminate the employee.

If you ever have occasion to believe that your personal safety is at risk and the risk is imminent, call corporate security or 911.

In his provocative book about behavior in the workplace Robert Sutton notes that:

The ability to gain control over little, seemingly trivial things is a hallmark of people who survive horrible and uncontrollable events including natural disasters or being a castaway, a hostage, or a prisoner of war.[17]

---

17 Robert I. Sutton, *The No Asshole Rule: Building a Civilized Workplace and Surviving One That Isn't* (New York: Hachette, 2007).

HEALTHY OUTLETS

Spotting our cars on the racetrack for the 2003 Zucchini Race,
with Mike Spalter, infrastructure chief (a la Jerry Garcia), on left
and me on the right, as the Princess of Darkness.

Sometimes all it takes to remove some of the tension from the workplace is a healthy outlet or two. At the bank, our team worked hard on this. One of our managers created a monthly birthday party to celebrate members of his team, and he bought a cake large enough to invite others in my overall group to attend as well. We had white-elephant gift exchanges in conjunction with holiday parties. We celebrated honors and awards that team members received.

Our most memorable event was the way we kicked off the annual United Way fundraising event with "The Zucchini Soapbox Races," a 16-year-old technology tradition where (as you can see) senior executives dressed up in odd costumes and competed against one another and employees for silly prizes.

I also invited members of the bank's leadership to attend our monthly all-hands meetings to make short presentations and answer questions from the team.

I wrote a weekly column that updated our team on news from the executive team, and celebrated their work in the past week. I tried to gather reports on outside events and conferences that team members had attended so that some of the high points could be shared with other team members.

Simpler, less organized and more personal strategies can break up the tensions in your workday. Take a walk at lunchtime, even if it is only around the block. Or hit the gym early in the morning. One of my colleagues used to meditate at either the garden near the top of the building or at the nearby library. Other employees went to the gym during their lunch hours or joined exercise classes offered on our work site.

Technology

Next to the people we work with, the most challenging part of our workplace is the technology. As technology has matured, we have come to take it for granted. When it's not available, we flounder. Like so many other parts of our lives, it's not until something terrible has happened that we learn to manage the risk, to ensure that we still have our data and can go on even if we lose our computers or other electronic devices.

When I owned and operated a computer company, technical support was available at the drop of a hat. Company servers were backed up daily onto other media, and if you had a technology problem, an engineer was personally available to troubleshoot and fix your problem.

Then I spent ten years at a large company, based in the technology group, and support was available, though not that quickly. Systems were backed up daily and corporate data was expected to be saved to servers, not to individual hard drives on desktop or laptop computers. Despite all the rules and protection around data at the bank, users still lost laptops, and found that in doing so, they had lost data they had saved to the local hard drive of the laptop rather than to the corporate server.

Today, my firm is housed in a office architected with secure wireless protocols, to minimize cables and technical clutter. Website support comes from a third party and from a contract with a large web-hosting company where most customers are large corporations. My office has no file server, and backups of corporate data are my own responsibility, handled through an online storage service. It is an entirely different world.

Whether you work in a large company with technical support or in a small company where it is assumed that you will handle your own data redundancy, it's worth it to understand clearly what the loss of data can represent: It may include passwords, confidential corporate client data, confidential personal data, or other files that are difficult to recreate with accuracy. The reasonable precautions recommended here can minimize your risk of data loss, for your company or yourself.

It is also worth it to familiarize yourself with the data policies of your company. Large corporations almost always have policies and practices established on the confidentiality of data that constitute intellectual property. If you work for a smaller company where such policies are not explicit, start backing up your personal data, and document how you do it, especially your own critical data.

In a large company, depending on the type of data classification policy, it may be illegal to email or otherwise expose to the external world content that belongs to your company. Even if you are simply communicating with another team member, it may be necessary to encrypt your communication. Check corporate policy in the area of data so that you do not inadvertently make a mistake that could cost you your job.

You should establish a backup routine for your personal data, which could include everything from photographs to financial information, and the "vital documents" discussed in Chapter I. I have gone through several stages of maturity for backups and now use continuous online storage as well as at least one of the other methods described here. I created folders on my home computer into which I save files but also save to an external cloud service. If files are important, I copy myself at another email address other than the one from which I am sending, to have another copy online.

If you cannot train yourself to regularly back up your data, then investigate online backup services[18], which can be configured in a variety of ways, including backing up your

18 Two of the most secure, well-known online backup services are provided by Apple iCloud and Carbonite.

data continuously or at particular times of the day. The cost of such a service is very affordable and relieves you of worrying that you need to perform backup operations. Regular checks of your online back-ups are advised.

———

Risk Tips 14, 15, 16, & 17

Make sure to maintain regular backups of your own data. Do not rely upon the company.

Store backups in a location other than your work area.

Do **not** create a consolidated password list and store it on your computer.

Set up security on all devices — including smartphones — so your data is safe if the device is stolen.

———

The contingencies you are planning for include the loss of your computer (while traveling, for instance), the theft of your computer, or the malfunction of your computer to the extent that you cannot use it. Having those files somewhere else means you can access them from another device.

Emergency Preparedness

Companies that reside in high-occupancy buildings are required by the Occupational Safety & Health Administration (OSHA) to educate and drill occupants on how to exit the building in case of a variety of emergencies. Many companies provide their employees with an emergency guide that highlights actions they should take in various situations. Those situations could include:

- Fire
- Medical emergencies
- Power outage
- Gas leaks
- Hazardous materials
- Suspicious substances
- Suspicious packages
- Bomb threats
- Workplace violence
- Civil unrest/riots
- Earthquakes
- Tornadoes

Employees should be provided with a list of emergency numbers to call, with 911 at the top for life-threatening emergencies. At the bank, we provided employees with stickers for their badges that contained the employee emergency-information-line number through which they could receive updates on facilities and closures, and instructions about whether to report to work. All employees were required to review the emergency management program once a year through an online training video.

Today many companies have an emergency alert system in place for their employees, to receive instant information on disruptions to the work environment. Be sure you take advantage of such alerts if your company offers them. If your company does not offer training or drills, make sure you act as your own risk detective and identify the locations where you could exit the building in the event of an emergency.

Sheltering in Place

Should something go wrong in the building, it is best to know in advance how you will handle the situation. At times when you will not be able to evacuate the building in which you are working, you may be asked to "shelter in place" rather than go home. Southern California employees at my former company, for example, would sometimes have to stay at work rather than go out into the heavy smoke from wildfires surrounding them. The best way to become self-sustaining in a situation like this is to put together an emergency kit and stash it in your office or cubicle, replenishing items from time to time. Imagine having to spend the night sleeping in your workspace — what would you want to have with you?

- Bottled water
- Protein or fruit bars
- Peanut or almond butter
- Dry cereal or granola
- Crackers
- Nuts
- Dried fruit
- Dried soup
- First-aid kit
- Extra medications
- Flashlight

In addition to food and first-aid supplies, think of clothing: Because I exercised near my office, I usually also had a gym bag that held extra clothes as well as toiletries. The items listed above are the ones I stockpiled in my office during the 10 years I spent at the bank.

Your cubicle or office contains other useful items. Just as a desk or table becomes the shelter you climb under in an earthquake, it can become a shelter against (for example) an armed shooter. At the bank each employee had a card that contained essential phone numbers for fire, police, and security, to which their own list of essential contacts could be added.

For the possibility that we would have to quickly evacuate the building rather than shelter in place, we drilled through fire-alarm tests to ensure that every employee knew where the exit doors for each floor were, so that they could leave by the stairs in case of a high-impact event.

Vital Work Documents

Every company provides different types of information to employees — your record at a company includes everything from your hire letter to your performance reviews and any HR-related documents. But your vital work documents also include a copy of your current résumé, as well as any complimentary letters you have received from executives, managers, or fellow workers. They are part of what I would call an "away kit," in case you decide to move to another company.

The list here is one I refined over years in the workplace, both as an employer and an employee. Some of these documents are useful for tax purposes, but you should keep others as evidence in case you ever need them in any form of arbitration with your employer.

Do keep your résumé updated at all times, including awards or citations you have received.

Do not leave these documents only at work or on your work computer; make copies and store them off-site.

Vital Work Documents
Your hire letter and any informational material included from HR

Any performance reviews that you have received

Professional recommendations

Awards, citations, or thank-you notes received from executives.

Any requests or plans for work improvement

Current copy of your résumé or curriculum vitae

List or photos of personal assets in your office or cubicle in case of loss

Chapter IV

On the Internet

There has been a rather continuous background digital buzz in our lives these past 10 years. We have become a nation of multi-taskers, juggling personal and professional responsibilities and at the same time seeking new and often adventuresome outlets for our energies. We are wired in, electronically, more hours of the day, continuing to engage after we leave the workplace.

Advances in technology have created unprecedented opportunities to organize schedules and information, and to shape our lives.

New social-media tools such as Twitter and websites like *The Huffington Post* and *Slate* aggregate information faster than any newspaper, magazine, or television news program can do, making it harder for us to put down the virtual connection and live our lives in person rather than on the internet. When we are asked to turn off our electronic devices, a type of low-level anxiety sets in. Sometimes it's simply a worry that we are not keeping up with our email, but other times it's a concern that by not being "always on," we are not real, or relevant.

Sophisticated technologies have invaded our personal space in other ways. The time we spend at home is in theory different than being in the office, but working remotely, from a home office or a coffee shop, is becoming a more frequent phenomenon. We take our devices everywhere. Sometimes we work and travel at the same time. Being "always on" can mean that we are living certain parts of our lives virtually.

Certainly technology has enabled simplified communications and a sense of connectedness to others. But as a result, our risk exposures have gone up. Personal safety is no longer just a matter of physical security — we live in several worlds. Each of us who spends time on the internet has developed a digital identity, and a string of passwords to go with different types of transactions. The business we transact on the internet can be compromised by hackers, whether it's a retail purchase or online banking session.

If you buy a car or a home, that transaction becomes part of a public record, available on the internet. As you make purchases on Amazon or eBay or other commercial sites, you lay down a more sophisticated set of database transactions. Though most such sites use "secure online banking," data leaks of your personal information are becoming more prevalent. Off the computer and on your person, there are other reasons to worry about data leaks: Many credit cards, most ATM cards, "enhanced" drivers licenses, and passports contain "Radio Frequency Identification Device" (RFID) technology, which means that data that is tracked and transferred can also be "sniffed" by hackers. The most straightforward solution is to house your information in a special wallet or passport holder that blocks transmissions via fabric that contains nickel and copper weaves.

We are acclimated to having a digital device — be it a cell phone, smartphone, laptop, or tablet computer — within close reach. A smartphone is used by many as a communications device, but also kept next to the bed as an alarm clock and a source of white noise. Many of us can hardly bear to put our digital devices down to drive the car. We are always on. This chapter looks at what risks are present when we are digitally tethered.

The internet has become the way we communicate rapidly with large numbers of friends and family. I use work and home laptops as well as an iPhone and an iPad4 in my work and travels. I have both personal and business identities on Facebook, Twitter, as well as a professional profile on LinkedIn. The world has changed rapidly from the time I used a typewriter to prepare my college application, which I mailed.

The '80s and '90s were an exciting time to be a PC/Windows user, and to build computer hardware, which is what my company, Delphi Computers & Peripherals, did from 1984 to 1999. We built personal computers and file servers to spec, installed Microsoft's operating system on the computers, and customized them with the applications needed to perform business functions such as database management and scientific, architectural, and medical applications. Most of our customers needed a modem and software to communicate, as well as what was then called an electronic-mail application, a word processor, and a spreadsheet to produce business documents.

Our customers ranged from professionals to developers, researchers and academicians who needed computers that were robust enough to do some of their work at home, to large companies with very specialized needs. Clients included architectural firms, biotechnical startups, a race track, medical institutions, the most unique bookstore and restaurant in Seattle, and both commercial and personal computers for the late Paul Allen.

The author James Gleick[19] would argue we should look back to jungle drums and later to Morse code as our earliest sources of information. But children today are amused and educated on devices whose ancestry is the PC. People of all ages know how to send emails and text messages, though not everyone is aware of what a digital footprint looks like or what it can mean.

Your Digital Identity

Technology has two faces: One is an enabler of communication and presence in the highly connected world in which we live; the other is a permanent record of your transactions over the internet.

In the early 1980s, I would create a single document — for example, an annual holiday letter or memo to staff on a computer and then print multiple copies.

Today, we can send customized emails to large groups, saving a great deal of time and individual effort. We can join a social network to which many of these same people on the holiday list belong — and update them with photos or

19 James Gleick, *The Information: A History, a Theory, a Flood* (New York: Pantheon Books, 2011).

status reports as often as we like.

It's certainly less time-consuming than writing and mailing individual letters. But in the rush to simplify our increasingly busy lives, we often forget what the internet has enabled.

As you use your computer to send and receive email, documents, and photographs, and participate in social networking sites like Facebook, you create a digital identity that may be more permanent than you think. This includes the email nickname that may have seemed cool for you at 16, but continues to follow you for years.

If you post your résumé on a job site like Monster, or list yourself on LinkedIn, the information on the résumé becomes available to a range of data-mining tools.

So the first thing to understand is that using the Internet makes it easy to find you, and find out about you, perhaps more than you wish others to know. If not protected, your information can become available for spammers and other electronic fraudsters.

The other thing to remember involves exercising a certain level of care and caution about what you post. It is not really possible to "erase" data that you create. As all of us who love investigative books and television shows such as NCIS know, your location can be traced when you are sending emails or calling on your cell phone.

A standard of care is a reasonable approach to take, especially in light of the rapidly emerging offers for online applications, delivered in the name of ease of use and simpler transactions. These applications are often easy for cyber thieves to hack into and steal your digital identity — thus the continuing focus by media on companies whose customer data has been "hacked." It is critical to make sure your operating system is up to date, with security patches installed. For many users to whom computer security is vitally important, it is worth considering aftermarket virus and web-browsing security programs such as Trend Micro, Sophos, or Norton Utilities, to silently monitor in the background for viruses, dangerous websites, and other forms of computer mischief.

Digital Threats

Email comes hard and fast at us these days and much of it needs to be sorted carefully and treated as a threat, even if you may have set up a spam filter on your computer. When we sign in on any given day, we might receive email with fake requests for help or even fake notices that we will have won large sums of money if only we send someone $20. The Department of Homeland Security has a list of what they call "Internet Hoaxes and Urban Legends"; you can find out more at *https://www.us-cert.gov/ncas/tips/ST04-009.*

Some of these emails may appear to come from your bank, asking you to sign in with login and password and provide your account number and Social Security number. It is important to note that, whether or not you have online banking set up, no bank will ever ask you for this information in this manner.

Most banks and major credit-card companies use the telephone or SMS/text alerts to contact you when it appears that you may be the victim of identity theft. You will of course want to regularly scan your credit-card and bank statements and call immediately if you note charges that you did not make. You can also contact the FBI's Internet Crime Complaint Center at *https://www.ic3.gov/crimeschemes.aspx.*

RESOURCES FOR COMPUTER, INTERNET-RELATED, AND INTELLECTUAL-PROPERTY CRIME[20]

Type of Crime	Appropriate Federal Investigative Law Enforcement Agencies
Computer intrusion (i.e., hacking)	FBI local office (www.fbi.gov) U.S. Secret Service (www.treasury.gov) Internet Crime Complaint Center (www.ic3.gov)
Password trafficking	FBI local office (www.fbi.gov) U.S. Secret Service (www.treasury.gov) Internet Crime Complaint Center (www.ic3.gov)
Counterfeiting of currency	U.S. Secret Service (www.treasury.gov)
Child pornography or exploitation	FBI local office (www.fbi.gov) Internet Crime Complaint Center (www.ic3.gov)

---

20 "Reporting Computer, Internet-Related, or Intellectual-Property Crime," The United States Department of Justice, updated December 18, 2018, https://www.justice.gov/criminal-ccips/reporting-computer-internet-related-or-intellectual-property-crime.

Type of Crime	Appropriate Federal Investigative Law Enforcement Agencies
Child exploitation and internet fraud matters that have a mail nexus	U.S. Postal Inspection Service (www.usps.com) Internet Crime Complaint Center (www.ic3.gov)
Internet fraud and spam	FBI local office (www.fbi.gov) U.S. Secret Service (Financial Crimes Division) (www.treasury.gov) Federal Trade Commission (www.ftc.gov) If securities-fraud or investment-related spam emails: Securities and Exchange Commission (www.sec.gov) Internet Crime Complaint Center (www.ic3.gov)
Internet harassment	FBI local office (www.fbi.gov)
Internet bomb threats	FBI local office (www.fbi.gov) ATF local office (www.atf.gov)
Trafficking in explosive/ incendiary devices or firearms over the internet	FBI local office (www.fbi.gov) ATF local office (www.atf.gov)

Finally, if you feel you are the victim of cyber stalking, you can report it to the Department of Justice at its Office for Victims of Crime, *www.ncvc.org*.

Best Internet Practices

I have set up all my computers and digital devices so that I must enter a password to have access to my programs and applications and email when I turn on the device. If my device is stolen or lost, no one can access the data on the computer without the password. I do not let the computer automatically "remember" my passwords for any Tom, Dick, or Harry to find if I leave my computer unattended.

I work from home using wireless access to the Internet, so I have installed an Internet router that is password protected with a unique password so that my encrypted mail and other transactions cannot be read by those driving by to sniff out such lucrative opportunities.

The key hardware in my office is the secure wireless router sitting to the left of the printer.

When I work from coffeehouses or other public locations, I always select a location that offers me that same type of internet access as I have at home. I also have installed state-of-the-art antivirus software that blocks spyware and malware as well. I routinely clear "remembered" passwords from my web browser by using the option "clear browsing history/data," especially before I take my laptop to a coffeehouse or public location to work.

I have my email and other accounts password protected. I have set the security settings on all my computers and applications so that I am automatically logged out and must log back in after a certain period of non-activity. I also change passwords on my computer and applications every six to eight months.

═══════════

Risk Tips 18, 19, 20, & 21

Install all browser updates

Install all operating system updates from Microsoft, Linux, or Apple.

Enable secure encrypted browsing — also called SSL — using *https:* rather than *http:* in setting up your computer and in security settings on social-media sites such as Facebook, where there is an option to do so.

In Facebook security settings, look at "login notifications" and check the box to receive an email when an unrecognized device tries to access your account.

═══════════

I utilize a continuous online cloud backup service for my computers, at a cost of less than $100 per year. It is a small price to pay for the peace of mind it offers against the risk that my computers might suffer a hardware failure or be lost or stolen.

I have purchased a license for anti-virus and anti-spam software that covers all my computers and renews every several years.

If I am using a public computer in a hotel or at a meeting, I am careful to log out when finished, so that no one who uses the computer after I am done has access to my information.

Though I never share files with others, I am aware that some users do. While this is a useful tool on a protected network, many people forget to "turn off" sharing capabilities when they join other networks such as at school or in a coffee shop. Files that are shareable are also open to theft.

Risk Tips 22, 23, 24, 25, & 26

In Facebook security settings, look at "login approvals" and check the box to have a security code sent to your phone to enable a remote login by an unrecognized device.

Avoid giving permission for third-party applications to access platforms such as Facebook. If you do give permission for programs like "Farmville," you have exposed your personal data to an external source.

Back up your computer files and photos via an online backup tool like Mozy or Carbonite.

Invest in a good antivirus program that also handles spyware and malware.

If you're running the Windows operating system, set up your computer to automatically receive security patches and updates from Microsoft.

Résumé and Job Searches

A résumé or its academic version, the curriculum vitae, is meant to be a brief summary of your contact information as well as your education and work experience, along with any papers or articles you've published. It's impossible to send a hiring recruiter a résumé without your basic contact information. For that reason, and because résumés tend to be submitted and stored electronically, you should be aware that such information can be data-mined on the Internet. Though your address and telephone number can be located in several ways, including property ownership searches through public databases, résumés that you create should be designed to provide the minimum amount of information that can be used for identity theft. There is never a good reason, for example, to put either your Social Security number or your passport number on a resume. Any agency that asks for your Social Security number is not to be trusted, unless they need it for federal reporting purposes.

Before you upload your résumés to either a corporate website or to larger sites such as *www.monster.com*, check to see what kind of security is in place on the site.

LinkedIn

LinkedIn is a business-related networking site launched in 2003. From its own statistics in May 2019, the site has more than 575 million users, with more than 260 million monthly active users. Of those LinkedIn users who are engaging with the platform monthly, 40 percent access it on a daily basis. Users register and create profiles, then invite business contacts to connect with them. Since the site includes both individuals and companies, employ ers can list jobs. The site is used heavily by HR recruiting managers to screen applicants for positions.

The site offers an easy way to keep in touch with former colleagues and to screen and then connect with interesting persons you meet professionally.

When you create a profile on LinkedIn or other business networking sites, write about yourself in the third person and be honest in your representation of previous experiences and the dates you served in earlier positions. Think twice about whether you wish to post a link on the business network to your personal blog or Facebook page. Remember that recruiters and managers alike can look at LinkedIn profiles and see whom you are connected to as well. Above all, remember that this is a professional networking site, now owned by Microsoft.

FACEBOOK

As of the first quarter of 2019, Facebook had 2.38 billion monthly active users. Many of us who thought we would never sign up for a Facebook account now find it to be a painless way to keep in touch with friends on a regular basis using our own words, links to articles, and posts of photos.

It appears that personal journals have been eclipsed by social media sites like Facebook or Twitter. A whole generation that finds email or instant messaging to be passé has moved to social media to communicate. And the line between personal and business lives has become increasingly blurred.

Facebook offers you the opportunity to simply create a profile and connect with your friends. You decide whether to become a frequent poster of photographs or status updates, or whether you only infrequently log in to see what your friends are doing.

The benefits of Facebook can be powerful if time is taken to adjust its security and privacy settings. Like Twitter, Facebook can be used as a powerful tool to organize and deliver information to thousands of people in the midst of great political turbulence, but the site is also a breeding ground for political disinformation. Both tools are increasingly used for emergency messages from the World Health Organization and the U.S. Centers for Disease Control, which have done most of their pandemic flu messaging using social media. The Federal Emergency Management Agency (FEMA) has started to identify social media as a key communications tool to both gather information from citizens and push it out in the midst of disasters.

We have seen how valuable Facebook and Twitter have been in allowing persons on the ground to notify relatives that they are safe in the midst of a disaster.

But in the business world, information on social media sites can also be retrieved and used for less than laudable purposes: to make decisions about whether persons will be admitted to college, be hired, be fired or be arrested. Employees are still being terminated for inappropriate posts on sites such as Facebook; in such posts they may have criticized their bosses, or perhaps even discussed the corporate culture, intellectual property, or new business projects.

The professional way to handle this risk is to be careful, very careful, what status updates or photographs you post — and be vigilant about un-tagging yourself in photos posted by friends if the photos portray you in a less-than-desirable situation. Be sure also that you regularly review your Facebook privacy settings to ensure that you are posting only to your friends rather than to the world. Facebook is not in fact a personal journal to be shared with the world — it may be a career killer or an invitation to forms of interaction or scrutiny that you really do not want.

On the truly negative side, we've read about a British Facebook user with more than 1,000 friends who announced she had taken pills and would be dead soon.[21]

This has happened so often now that Facebook offers advice on how to take action if you read suicidal content. Recently, Facebook has begun to use artificial intelligence tools to detect posts that might indicate that the user is suicidal. Such posts are reviewed and then help is dispatched if necessary. One of the first actions that law enforcement will take is to double-check a victim's Facebook site to understand potential causes of a murder or suicide. We know too that extremists often post videos, photos, and ramblings on sites like Facebook. In the summer of 2011, Norwegian police were able to understand a great deal from examining

---

21   Dave Masko, "Facebook's Dark Side: Suicides, Leaks and Controlling User Content," Huliq, updated January 7, 2011, http://www.huliq.com/10282/facebook-dark-side-suicides-leaks-and-controlling-user-content.

emails as well as Facebook posts for Anders Behring Brei-
vik, the accused extremist Norwegian assassin.

There is no doubt that Facebook and Twitter have also
shaped new generations of voters, politicians, and coa-
li-tions. There seems to be no cause that is too complex to
try to raise money for or mobilize fans for on Facebook.
From a security perspective, Larry Kaminer from Personal
Security Group has a series of tips for those who frequently
post on Facebook. He advises that posts should be made,
whenever possible, after the fact of an event, with certain
details left vague. He warns about "checking in" and an-
nouncing where you are via location-based services (such as
in "I'm at Westminster Abbey in London") because criminals can use the detail in those posts to know you are away
from home and thus target you or your home for a burglary. At the end of his blog on this topic he notes that:

> *You might think that only friends and family in your so-
> cial media network are privy to anything you share. You
> also might think that your friends have vetted the friends
> they share their platforms with. Think again!* A Reuters
> *article on a British company, Legal & General, published
> some statistics from a study they did several years ago. Their
> study revealed that only 13% of Facebook users vetted a
> friend request and a staggering 92% accepted new follows
> on Twitter without doing any checks!!* [22]

Like on LinkedIn, both people and organizations can have
pages on Facebook or Twitter. I have a personal account

[22] "Online Safety and Social Media Security Awareness," The Personal Safety Training Group, updated July 27, 2011, https://www.
personalsafetygroup.com/2011/07/social-media-safety-and-security/.

limited to friends, as well as a corporate account where I deliver brand risk messages on both Facebook and Twitter. I try to remain aware that I am promoting my brand on both sites, and try to be careful not to share political opinions or discuss inflammatory issues in such a public context.

TWITTER

Twitter is a social-networking site that allows its users to send and receive messages called "tweets" — text-based messages each delivered in 280 words or less and displayed on the pages of the author and those who follow them. With more than 330 million monthly active users worldwide as of the first quarter of 2019, this tool cannot be underestimated. How much can be said in 280 words!

We have a few colorful examples of how tweeting can go terribly wrong, and very public, photos and all. Our most notorious example is former Congressman Anthony Weiner, who ABC News reported "panicked after he sent what he thought was a private tweet with an image attached — and then realized he had actually made it public, available to thousands of his Twitter followers."[23] Weiner's mistake might be yours one day, unless you realize that these social-media tools are public forums, not private networks.

On the positive side, tweets can be used to deliver broad public health messages across the globe. The World Health Organization (WHO) learned from monitoring Twitter

23 Ned Potter, "Congressman Weiner: How Not to Use Twitter?," ABC News, June 8, 2011, https://abcnews.go.com/Technology/congressman-anthony-weiner-twitter-social-media-make-sexting/story?id=13783677.

feeds that victims of the 2011 Honshu earthquake and tsunami were purchasing iodine, a wound cleaner, to dose themselves orally against nuclear radiation. WHO was able to deliver a clear message using both Facebook and Twitter that the iodine would not help and in fact was poisonous. The data shows a clear drop in this behavior after the WHO posts and tweets.

Smartphones

In the past decade, the smartphone — in particular the iPhone and BlackBerry — has revolutionized our ability to communicate, linking our life and work on a device that fits in the pocket.

On a BlackBerry supplied by my employer for ten years, I could be anywhere in the world and yet virtually connected as chair of the bank's crisis management team. That reduced a significant amount of risk for the company. I was just returning from Ireland in 2003 when the East Coast blackout took place, but stayed connected with the team as it became clear the blackout would not spread via underwater cables to Europe.

On my iPhone today I appreciate the advantages of having free applications, though I know that there is a cost to the data gathered on me and my habits.

I use Apple's iPad primarily for the extensive reading I do. In one of his technology columns in the *Wall Street Journal*, Walt Mossberg pointed me to an application called QuickOfficePro that runs on the iPad that allows you to read and edit documents created in Microsoft Office programs.

Other platforms extend the scope of smartphones, particularly with the Android and Microsoft operating systems available on many models.

I have a university laptop as well as another laptop that I use for business connected to ASA. Both use Windows-based operating systems.

OTHER SMART DEVICES

Technology has leapfrogged over security and privacy concerns in the past several years, thanks to the "Internet of Things" (IoT) and smart devices – sensors that can gather and store enormous amounts of data about you (example: Fitbit), your home (example: Amazon's Cloud Cam and Ring), and your tastes and habits, including purchasing habits (Amazon's Echo is a good example). In order to get to "know you," such devices collect data that could in fact be subpoenaed in a court case. Other challenges include questions around how such devices get patched for security vulnerabilities; or whether what is a generic password can be changed. We are at early stages where managing multiple devices across the Internet of Things is possible without subjecting one's digital identity to additional privacy incursions.

APPLICATIONS

Before you download an application to your computer or smart device, please take the time to do a search for reviews and comments on the application and its safety.

Installing anti-virus software to your smartphone is also a good idea.

Be careful with turning on "location services." Make sure to turn it on only for vital applications such as maps. Do you really want everyone to know where you are all the time?

Finally, take the time to back up the data on your smart device as well as your laptops. The device you are making phone calls on is also at least as powerful as an entire computer.

Vital Internet Documents

It may not seem that you would need to keep copies of bills of sale or other details on license agreements, but it takes only one instance where you need to replace a computer or other device to find out that it is hard to make an insurance claim or transfer a software license without such information.

All of this connectedness — through both devices and applications — creates risk that is manageable by taking thoughtful precautions. Identifying your vulnerable areas is the first step to handling risks. The reasonable precautions provided in this chapter outline some of the ways you can begin to minimize the risk, even if the device is lost or stolen.

Vital Internet Documents

Bills of sale for computers and other electronic devices, including warranty information and serial numbers, including smart IoT devices you install in your home

License-agreement numbers for such items as antivirus software or online backup

Copies of purchase agreements on applications, including serial numbers and secure location for storing copies of DVDs/CDs

Chapter V

On the Road

Traveling is an acquired skill. There's no doubt that, for many, the idea of leaving home triggers dual feelings of excitement and fright. Remember Archie Bunker, who rarely left his recliner, much less Queens? The idea of going to a place that is unfamiliar, where people speak a different language, where you don't know the rules, can be intimidating. Americans are not always viewed with open arms. But when you weigh the risks against the rewards, travel offers a means to find out more about yourself than is possible in any other context. Travel can lower the barriers between cultures, making us more aware of our similarities than our differences.

So far, we've looked at how to identify and handle risks at home, at school, at work, and online. Those environments are all familiar and usual to us in a way that travel is not. We all have known locations, habits, and practices in the first four environments. The fifth — travel — is the outlier on the risk spectrum.

Familiar routines have disappeared, and we have to make many more judgments about the right or wrong thing to do. We begin to see just how much we are not in charge of, how much we do not know.

If we are visiting a country where English is not the primary language, then we may be so busy trying to make ourselves understood that we fail to pay attention and manage potential threats. If we become appreciative of what we are seeing or doing, we tend to drop our guard and sometimes lose our common sense as well.

Here I will identify the most common risks that we face when we travel. From the discussion of each risk, you'll be able to extract your own list of reasonable precautions that is customizable for any travel situation you encounter.

Dropping Your Guard

I grew up in a small town in Iowa. It was not until I had nearly finished my undergraduate degree that I took the train from Iowa City to Chicago. I will never forget the joy of that first piece of travel to an unknown place. I was making the trip to see a once-in-a-lifetime exhibition at the Art Institute of Chicago — a traveling show of paintings and drawings of the great French Impressionist, Henri Matisse.

To this day I remember the large canvases framed in golden wood, and the beautiful drawings. Hung in nearby galleries were other Impressionists from the Art Institute's own strong collection. Over the years I have revisited those galleries whenever I am in Chicago.

In that same trip, I also made a tour of used bookstores and bought books. The whole trip was almost an out-of-body experience for me. Though I was alert, the notion of personal safety on the streets of Chicago was the last thing on my mind. I was lucky that I did not have my pockets picked.

Compare that to a later situation in New York City in the 1980s, where I was walking down the street with my husband and a friend. I was clowning around, not paying attention. I wore a shoulder bag, which I opened to pull out my sunglasses. I did not re-zip the bag and, as a result, my wallet was stolen. Unless it has happened to you, it's hard to imagine the combination of fear and rage that is provoked when you lose all evidence of your identity as well as your cash and credit cards. Fortunately, I have a good memory and my husband carried the same credit cards as me, so we were able to report the loss of the cards rapidly. It was my first experience of being targeted, and I did not like it one bit. I like to believe the best about people, and this caused me to become overly paranoid for a while. Interestingly enough, once we were home from the conference, we received a call from a good Samaritan who had found the wallet with everything but the money still in it. At his own expense, he mailed it to us, a reminder — which I have seen over and over since then — that there are good people in the world.

This is less a caution to be careful with your purse or wallet as it is a reminder to remain alert when you are in an unfamiliar environment, whether it's a new city or an unfamiliar parking garage late at night.

Too Much Luggage

I have never really understood why there are so many travelers still standing in long lines with two or three large bags to check. Where are they going? Why would they need to take so much stuff? Is it because they think they cannot find what they need at their destination? Or do they have some deep-seated desire to be well-dressed in the eyes of people they probably will never see again? Once they have hauled this mass of luggage to their first destination, it's too late to lighten their load for this round of travel. That's why I am a great fan of Rick Steves's packing test: Pack your bag and then wear it or carry it around with you for a day or so until you add and subtract what you thought was essential, to get optimum weight.[24]

Because of the length of the trip and a longish layover in Miami, I decided to check my bag through when my friend Jenny and I accepted an offer to visit our friend Luba in Buenos Aires in 2000. I did all my research on the city itself so that I'd be comfortable moving around on my own. When my friend Pablo asked me to deliver a new 35mm camera to Luba, I said of course, and packed the camera into my checked bag. In retrospect, I should have known that this was a poor idea — and if I'd done my reading on cautions having to do with customs or transporting personal property, I'd have known that it is never a good idea to pack expensive items — whether clothing, jewelry, or cameras — into a checked bag. Of course when I retrieved my bag, the locks had been tampered with and the camera was gone. Fortunately, a receipt for the camera as well

24 Rick Steves, "Packing Smart and Traveling Light," Rick Steves' Europe, accessed August 21, 2019, https://www.ricksteves.com/travel-tips/packing-light/packing-smart.

as insurance coverage meant that eventually Luba did get her camera. But I've never forgotten the lesson behind that story: Do not check your bag if you can avoid it. If you do check your bags, carry your valuables separately.

I took just two bags on a month-long train trip in 2009.

Today, I travel with one rolling suitcase not quite full. I add a lightweight briefcase into which goes my wallet, cosmetics bag, and a plastic file with printouts of boarding pass and hotel confirmation. To stay connected, I add a small laptop or iPad that have been fully charged. If traveling internationally, I also carry several power adapters to cover my electronic devices and an additional fully-charged battery for my laptop.

I minimize my risk of loss and save fees by carrying my bag onboard and fitting it into the overhead compartment on the plane. My briefcase goes on the floor by my feet for easy access. I do not carry a purse because of carry-on restrictions, though I do have a flat one packed in my bag, so I am not stuck only with a briefcase during my travels.

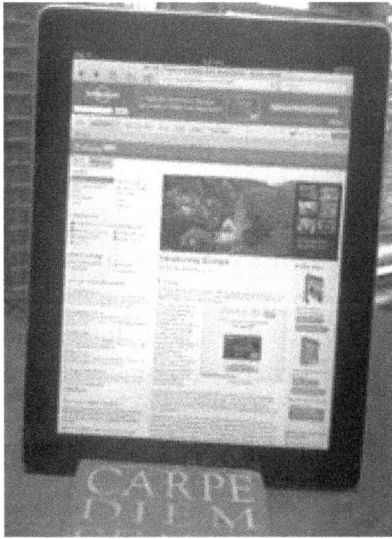

My iPad2 allows me to easily carry maps and reference guides.

In addition to the research you will already have done about your destination before you leave home, you can continue absorbing information about it via electronic devices that have replaced heavy travel books. You can carry applications on your digital device that offer maps and city guides, and often the same content as in the books.[25]

Not Being Prepared
"Be prepared" means recognizing that you could lose your wallet, have your jewelry make you a target on the street, or not have access to laundry or dry-cleaning services. So

25 Lonely Planet is certainly one of the most popular sites for me and many others. Its smartphone application can be found at https://www.lonelyplanet.com/guides.

in addition to paring down what you carry, it's necessary to make copies of your critical travel documents. Before I leave, I make two photocopies of my passport, credit cards, health-insurance card, and any travel insurance I have purchased. I identify an emergency contact and give that person my itinerary and other relevant information. At the same time, I gather all the phone numbers I might need on the road, including that of the U.S. Embassy and any other emergency numbers that might apply, including for my travel insurance. If I have any special medical conditions, I make sure I have a doctor's letter with me that documents them that I could hand it to a doctor in another country. And for international flights, a good idea is to go online and register your trip through the U.S. Department of State's "Smart Traveler Enrollment Program" at *https:// step.state.gov/step*.

One photocopy of my documents stays in the file at home and the other stays tucked into my suitcase in case my wallet is stolen. I make sure that the serial numbers of any electronic device I am carrying are stored online. My packing plan is always to wear outfits more than once and to be able to mix and match. Because I love to walk, I have a good pair of walking shoes that I wear rather than pack. Anything I take to wear can be hand washed or cleaned on the road. I leave all my fancy jewelry or flashy clothing at home, so that I do not become an easy target on the street. Per one of Rick Steves' tips,[26] if I were single I would invest in a cheap wedding ring to wear, particularly in countries where men are more aggressive than they are here.

26 Rick Steves, "Extra Tips for Women Traveling Solo," Rick Steves' Europe, accessed August 21, 2019, https://www.ricksteves.com/travel-tips/trip-planning/tips-for-solo-women-travelers.

Vital Travel Documents
Passport
International driver's license
Debit or credit card(s)
Emergency contact information
Health-insurance card
Travel-insurance document
Doctor's letter to cover any special medical condition

Some countries do not allow access to certain sites, such as Facebook or Twitter. Know which sites are prohibited before you leave home.

Finally, make sure you have notified your bank and credit card companies that you will be traveling internationally so that charges are validated but not refused.

By this time, you will already have done the research to know whether or not you need a visa to enter the country, and how far in advance you need to apply for it. The same is true of shots or vaccinations you might need. Take care of these matters in a timely fashion so you are not worried at the last minute.

Being Bankrupted by Your Phone Bill
If you are traveling on business with a corporate smart-phone or cell phone, the costs of calls you make and emails

or downloads will be borne by your employer — or you will have been cautioned about what the company will pay for and what not. Most corporate plans have an option to turn on international travel.

If you are paying your own communications bill, you'll want to minimize roaming fees, which apply when you use the device outside the contracted service area. If you will be making local calls from your new location, you might consider getting an "unlocked" cell phone that can handle prepaid SIM cards purchased in the country where you are traveling.[27]

Checklist of Travel Websites

Government Resources
Centers for Disease Control: www.cdc.gov/travel
Smart Traveler Enrollment Program: travelregistration.state.gov
Transportation Security Administration (TSA): www.tsa.gov
U.S. Customs & Border Protection: www.cbp.gov
U.S. Department of State: www.travel.state.gov

Travel Insurance Comparisons
Insure My Trip: www.insuremytrip.com

Other Resources for the Independent Traveler
Lonely Planet: www.lonelyplanet.com
LP Message Board: https://www.lonelyplanet.com/thorntree/
BootsnAll Travel Network: www.bootsnall.com
Rick Steves' Europe Through the Back Door: www.ricksteves.com
New York Times Travel: www.nytimes.com/section/travel
Wall Street Journal, "The Middle Seat":
https://www.wsj.com/news/types/the-middle-seat

---

27 For a thorough discussion, see Michelle Higgins, "The High Costs of Dialing Abroad," *New York Times* August 7, 2011.

Another option is to use an internet phone service such as Skype to make free calls to anyone who also has Skype on his or her computer. Skype makes its application available on smartphones as well, in case you are not carrying a laptop.

Think carefully about how many files you carry on your computer, in particular if many of them belong to your company. Privacy rules are not as strong in some countries as they are in the United States.

Looking Like a Target

A number of reasonable precautions fall into this section.

One is to not be caught at odd hours in areas that might not be safe or that are not heavily trafficked. Adjust your schedule if necessary, so that you are sightseeing during the times of day when the maximum number of people are out.

The next would be to reiterate: Don't wear flashy jewelry or expensive clothes that identify you as a target. If you are carrying electronics, don't flaunt them.

This also includes speaking with care and thoughtfulness — trying hard not to be culturally insensitive when you encounter customs or practices that are different from your own. Learn basic phrases: "hello," "help," "where is the restroom?" and "thank you." Although you may not be fluent in their language, most residents will appreciate that you are trying to learn their language rather than assuming that everyone speaks English.

Especially if you are traveling alone, and even more particularly if you are a woman traveling alone, it's essential that you do your research.

The Mideast, for example, holds special challenges for women. A colleague who speaks Arabic with an English accent found herself the target of an irate Mideast citizen when she walked down the street to pick up a package in her professional work clothes, wearing makeup and without wearing a head covering. Dressing like her American self in this case meant that she was therefore mistaken for a prostitute by a female in an upper-level apartment, who first hurled curses at her and then an open can of tomato soup. No cab driver would pick up my colleague, looking as she did, like a prostitute who had just been punished properly. She says she was lucky not to have been arrested by the police or detained.

When walking on the street, walk with confidence, having studied your maps before you leave your hotel. Make sure that your handbag or pack is closed and carried close to your body. Remain alert, and follow your instincts. In some countries, pickpockets are as likely to be children or women as men. And men are equal targets for criminals.

Getting Lost

Something like 65 percent of women have made solo trips in this country or abroad. If you are traveling to another country, particularly a country where you may not be familiar with its customs, advance research and study of the culture means that you will not be constrained when you travel. A terrific website to check out is *https://solotraveler-*

world.com/about/solo-travel-statistics-data/.

Personally, I've had only one bad experience traveling on my own, in St. Petersburg, Russia. It's illustrative of many of the risks I've already discussed.

My husband was speaking at an international conference, and I chose to walk from our hotel north along the city's most vibrant thoroughfare, the Nevsky Prospeckt. I enjoyed window shopping, street musicians, and folk art displays on the Prospeckt, as well as the combined smells of diesel fuel and cigarettes that seemed to stamp their imprint on my recollections of the city.

From the Neva River bridge, St. Petersburg, 2006.

I had a wonderful lunch about halfway to the conference location at the Grand Hotel Europa, the most expensive hotel in the heart of the city, and then decided to take a cab the rest of the way. From my reading I knew that I should negotiate the cab fare in advance, so I selected a well-maintained cab directly in front of the hotel, on the assumption that it would be a safe cab since it was in front of this very expensive hotel.

When I realized the cab driver did not speak English, perhaps a flag should have gone up. I showed the driver the address, to which he nodded yes. I negotiated the fare with him, and off we went. The language barrier would prove to be a larger risk than I had anticipated.

I knew we were traveling the right direction because we crossed the bridge in the photo, and to the right I could see The Hermitage. He swung left and pulled up in front of a building that, as far as I could tell, said "Museum" in Cyrillic. I tried to say "not the right address" to him, pointing at the address on the envelope, but he gestured me out of the cab. I got no help inside the museum, which infuriated me, and so I went back out on to the main arterial and tried to find someone who spoke English. It seemed like an eternity, but fortunately I was able to get directions within ten minutes from a student.

This was the only time I've ever been worried while traveling about what I might have gotten myself into. I had no idea how to catch a cab back to the hotel in case I could not find the conference site. I did not know how to contact the police for assistance, or whether it would be a good idea. I had not realized how few people spoke English in the most cosmopolitan city in Russia. No red flags appeared until it was too late. I had done a very sloppy job of research.

Learning from my past experiences, now I always carry a business card from my hotel with me, in case I cannot make myself understood about where I wish to go.

Losing Your Digital Self

If you need to check your email or make posts to social networks, locate secure, password-protected Wi-Fi locations in public places. It is worth it to pay a fee to use a secure location; still, make sure you sign on and off if you use a public computer. Ensure that you have installed a strong security program.[28] I do not recommend using online banking or other financial programs in any type of insecure location.

Illness

If you are on company business, you may be covered by health insurance that your employer provides. Do review that insurance with an eye to supplementing it if it won't cover all the contingencies you are concerned about.

One of the best-known travel insurance programs for individuals or employers is offered by a company called SOS Insurance. Individuals traveling without business protection or who worry that their existing medical insurance might not cover international incidents can also purchase this coverage or travel insurance provided by other carriers. SOS Insurance coverage includes evacuating you from the country you are visiting, if necessary, and also covers a range of medical situations. For this or other coverage you are reviewing, do pay careful attention to exclusions on the insurance for either pre-existing conditions or for injuries

[28] There are many security applications available; I use Trend Micro's Titanium, which claims to authenticate any wireless hot spot or Wi-Fi network.

during a range of activities such as:

- caving
- mountaineering or rock climbing
- skydiving
- parachuting
- bungee-jumping
- ballooning
- hang gliding
- martial arts
- rallying
- racing
- any kind other than on foot[29]

Other forms of travel insurance are provided by companies such as MedjetAssist, for which you can find comparative reviews on insuremytrip.com (see footnote). MedjetAssist, for example, will actually evacuate you quickly to the hospital or critical-care facility of your choice in this country.

While you're looking into travel or extra medical insurance, also review health information on your destination available from the Centers for Disease Controls at *www.cdc.gov/travel*. The CDC site is also the location where you can learn about any vaccines you might need before you travel. Some vaccines need to be injected several months before departure.

---

29 The list is longer than I have shown here — more proof of the importance of reading the fine print. You can find reviews of SOS and the other major travel insurance providers at Insure My Trip: www.insuremytrip.com

Detention or Arrest

International travel means observing the security policies and standards established by both our government and the host government. If you pack in such a way that you have ignored the rules — with large bottles of cosmetics or with your favorite hunting knife — you run the risk of being detained or arrested before you leave the ground. Read the guidelines posted by the Transportation Security Administration (TSA) at *www.tsa.gov* to understand of what you may or may not carry in your onboard and/or checked luggage, and the screening procedures you will be subjected to at the airport, especially if you have any special medical conditions. In some locations, particularly in Asia, rules for the possession of unlicensed drugs can be unimaginably grim: Don't risk it.

Visit the U.S. Customs & Border Patrol site (*www.cbp.gov*) to understand what travel documents you will need to travel to other countries or to return to the United States.

Make note of the location of the U.S. Embassy at your destination and read on the Department of State site *travel.state.gov* just what the embassy can do or not do to assist you if you are detained or arrested in the country. Together with your research on the Department of State's website, you should be able to move smoothly through security.

If by any chance your flight is cancelled or rescheduled because you were detained by airport officials, it pays to know what your rights are and how to proceed.[30]

30 See Scott McCartney, "Room Service in Terminal B," *Wall Street Journal*, January 20, 2011. https://www.wsj.com/articles/SB10001424052748703951704576091923287595948. McCartney writes

KIDNAPPING AND HOSTAGE-TAKING

The Department of State's website provides extensive information on countries where your risk may be higher, and where threats such as kidnapping or hostage-taking are prevalent.

> *"Travel Advisories are issued when long-term, protracted conditions that make a country dangerous or unstable lead the State Department to recommend that Americans avoid or consider the risk of travel to that country. A Travel Advisory is also issued when the U.S. Government's ability to assist American citizens is constrained due to the closure of an embassy or consulate or because of a drawdown of its staff."*[31]

Once you know where you are going, check the list of countries where your risk is extraordinarily high, and/ or where you do not necessarily receive assistance from the U.S. Embassy.

FAILURE TO BECOME A MORE INTERESTING PERSON

If art helps me understand the world through time, then travel is what makes me a citizen of the world.

Both art and travel multiply what I know, what I see, and what I understand, especially about peoples and cultures that are different from my own.

Before I travel, and while I am on the road, I try to study

---

a regular column called "The Middle Seat" that is always good.

31 "Planning Your Trip," Foreign Agricultural Service, United States Department of Agriculture, accessed August 21, 2019, https://www. fas.usda.gov/international-travel/planning-your-trip.

the area I'm visiting, to understand as much as I can about the country's culture, its art and architecture, as well as a bit about its politics.

This photo here is of our son, James, and me in France in 2002. He was on a tour with the Roosevelt High School Jazz Band, performing at the North Sea, Montreaux, and San Sebastian jazz festivals and making other civic appearances along the way. Since the band was to play in the Luxembourg Gardens in Paris, I flew to Paris and vacationed for ten days. I was able to explore the city in depth in the days surrounding his visit and spend time with the band as well.

With our son in Versailles, in 2002.

We spent nearly four hours in the gardens of Versailles, amazed at the complexity and beauty that had been designed centuries ago, against one of the most completely over-the-top palaces ever built. That palace is now a museum with thousands touring it every year. We arrived with the rest of the band on its tour bus after having done a quick tour of Paris proper along the way. Students were free to look on their own, and then take the train back into the city. That such tours have been part of any trip that the band's director, Scott Brown, designs is entirely in keeping with Brown's own philosophy about music and about giving back, wherever you go, and absorbing at the same time the cultures, customs, and music of the host country. In planning this trip or others, Brown ensured that his band had safe but genuinely unforgettable cultural experiences in locations that ranged from Lincoln Center in New York City, to the Great Wall of China, to the funky jazz houses of New Orleans.

That combination of travel and cultural education paid off, at least for my son. Since then, he's been back to Paris and in Bosnia, Croatia, Serbia, and Sweden for study. Having traveled so much early in his life, he is comfortable in many places in the world. And through the experience of early travel with the jazz band, he learned how to remain watchful and yet enjoy himself wherever he is.

And that's the point, isn't it? Travel isn't just getting on a tour bus or ticking off locations in a tour guide. Travel makes you a citizen of the world, a more interesting person. I like to think back on the Paris trip as the one where I really did the research before I left home. Several friends loaned me books, and I did a fair amount of online research, including on how I would get around in the city. I booked a small hotel in Montmartre that was less than a block from the underground Metro system. Though the hotel had no elevator, it was scrupulously clean and served guests from many countries, and included a morning breakfast of coffee or tea and croissants.

A friend had advised me that the French were a courteous people if Americans would only slow down long enough to say "Bonjour" before they fired off their questions. As a result of remembering that piece of advice, I was treated warmly wherever I went in Paris. I tried to blend in as much as possible, using the Metro for all my travel in the city. I carried a slim volume that grouped attractions by neighborhood and showed me how to link them on a walk. Every evening on my way back to the hotel, I picked up my dinner at a local shop to enjoy in my room with a book, or poring over maps to plan the following day.

I wanted to investigate Paris in detail so I limited myself to only one trip in the countryside outside the city, to see the home and gardens of the great Impressionist painter, Claude Monet. Getting from Paris to Giverny could not have been easier. I simply took the Metro to the stop for the Gare Saint-Lazare, a train station that has not changed much since Monet painted it in 1877. The train ride to Vernon was uneventful, and a small tour bus took us into the countryside to Giverny, where roughly 500,000 people visit each year in the months that it is open.

My detective work paid off. The experience of walking through Monet's home, workshop, and gardens is not one I will ever forget. I was carrying a small 35mm camera. I had known Monet's work from his paintings shown in various collections in this country. Being there enabled me to see what he painted through my own eyes. He designed two gardens, one of which included the lily pond in my photo. The gardens offered him subject matter for his paintings for twenty years. It is possible to spend a whole day in those gardens simply to record the names of the trees, bushes, and flowers that live there in the faint hope that one's own gardens might be improved from having seen Giverny and the small neighborhood less than one hundred yards away — a hotel where Monet put up his friends when they came to visit, and a beautiful museum situated among the hay stacks and hills.

At Giverny, Claude Monet's home, in 2002.

I left Paris a happy woman, having seen everything on my list and more. The research had paid off. I had managed my risks well. I knew I would come back because there is more to learn. I said goodbye to Paris from another great station, the Gare du Nord, where I picked up the train that took me to the airport.

Paris had made me a more interesting person. The trip to Giverny had a lasting impression: In 2013, never having had a drawing or painting class, I started to take a water-color class with Jan Morris, in part as a way to open up a new path. I took classes with her for several years, until I started to teach full time. I am happy to report that I have returned to three-hour watercolor classes this past spring with painter Sandra Kahler, who is convinced that I can learn to draw, and paint, both of which will be a conse-quence of my visit to Giverny.

Seattle's Union Station was gateway to my 2009 train trip.

You have probably deduced by now that I love trains and train stations, above and below ground. My last sto-ry brings us full circle and illustrates how it is possible to think through one's risks and make a consequential plan. I had left my position at JPMorgan Chase in the spring of

2009 after transitioning the company-wide programs I'd been responsible for at Washington Mutual. I was tired. Though not as anxious as some who wondered where their next job would come from, I knew I needed to come to a conclusion on various options I'd been exploring for the past six months. I bought a thirty-day rail pass, and paid extra for a private sleeper compartment on the longer routes. I mapped out a journey that would take me from the West Coast to the East Coast, to spend time with people who knew me well. I was able to route myself through Santa Fe to take part in a weekend workshop called "Reboot Your Life," which helped me look twice at the risks and opportunities I had been considering.[32]

Though Amtrak provides internet access on its trains today, I was delighted to be unplugged for that trip, because I could think and sleep and write as the urge came upon me. My discussions with those I visited were without boundaries or schedule. By the time I arrived back in Seattle, I had settled on my course. I would open a risk-consulting firm where I could think and write about risk and innovation while at the same time offering world-class risk assessment services. I described myself as a risk detective in my first television-news interview.

And the rest, as they say, is history.

This book has addressed a series of reasonable precautions to reduce risks at home, at school, at work, online, and on

---

32 The workshop is offered several times a year by the authors of a book by the same name. Catherine Allen, Nancy Bearg, Rita Foley, and Jaye Smith, *Reboot Your Life: Energize Your Career and Life by Taking a Break* (Beaufort Books, 2011).

the road without slowing our forward momentum.

That last story is designed, like the others, to show that risk-taking is an essential part of personal growth. Change of any kind is risky and often takes us out of our comfort zones, the habits, practices, and ways of looking at the world that seem second nature.

You may wonder if things can be different, whether personal change is possible. I say yes. And that's where this book can help you take some simple, inexpensive steps forward: By becoming more aware of the world, you are already managing more risk. By looking closely into these five areas of your life — at home, at school, at work, online, and on the road — you can build solutions that are tailored to your own circumstances.

I wish you a life that is filled with light and possibilities, with risks managed and plans well made.

Appendix

Checklist of Risk Tips

1. Secure your home, then purchase an appropriate amount of homeowner's insurance.

2. Create a household inventory in case your home is damaged.

3. Ensure that your most valuable records are portable and stored in at least two different places.

4. Create both an emergency management plan for your family to follow and an emergency kit that will allow you to live off the grid for three to five days.

5. Do your own homework on care providers. Obtain references and check them.

6. Does the school you are looking at have a special focus? Can you speak with the teachers and form a preliminary opinion about fit?

7. If your child is considering a sports team or jazz band or theater group, can you perform a version of a background check on the person who will coach them? Given the cases of coaching abuse in the news, this seems especially important.

8. Reread the discussion on how to create an emergency plan for your family that is in Chapter 1. Then be sure your child knows how to reach you or where to meet you if it is not possible to meet at home.

9. If your child has never ridden on public transit, make this an experience the two of you can share, so that your child gets a look at the bus environment with you along the first time.

10. When your children are born, make a strategic plan for how your family will handle the expense of college.

11. Ensure that your children are making decisions on their own, with your guidance, from an early age. If they already make independent decisions, they have precedent for how to handle new challenges in college.

12. The habits that you form in college will remain with you most of your life. Be conscious and modify habits that do not lead to success.

13. After you do the informal research, report suspicious or inappropriate behavior at work. Document in your own words both the incident and the date you reported it.

14. Make sure to maintain regular backups of your own data. Do not rely upon the company.

15. Store backups in a location other than your work area.

16. Do not create a consolidated password list and store it on your computer.

17. Set up security on all devices — including smartphones — so your data is safe if the device is stolen.

18. Install all browser updates.

19. Install all operating-system updates from Microsoft, Linux, or Apple.

20. Enable secure encrypted browsing — also called SSL — using *https:* rather than *http:* in setting up your computer and in security settings on socialmedia sites such as Facebook, where there is an option to do so.

21. In Facebook security settings, look at "login notifications," and check the box to receive an email when an unrecognized device tries to access your account.

22. In Facebook security settings, look at "login approvals" and check the box to have a security code sent to your phone to enable a remote login by an unrecognized device.

23. Avoid giving permission for third-party applications to access platforms such Facebook. If you do give permission for programs like "Farmville," you have exposed your personal data to an external source.

24. Back up your computer files and photos via an online backup tool like Mozy or Carbonite.

25. Invest in a good antivirus program that also handles spyware and malware.

26. If you're running the Windows operating system, set up your computer to automatically receive security patches and updates from Microsoft.

Your Emergency Kit

Water: One gallon per person per day, three to fourteen days' worth
Food: Nonperishable, including food for special diets
First Aid Kit: One for home, one for car
Cash: In small bills, enough for three to five days

Tools:
- Eating utensils, including can opener and utility knife
- Battery-operated radio, extra batteries
- Flashlight(s), extra batteries
- Small sewing kit
- Compass and whistle
- Matches in waterproof container
- Wrench to shut off gas and water
- Work gloves
- One or more signal flares
- Rope ladder near second-story exit
- Plastic bucket
- Disinfectant, bleach, liquid detergent
- Battery-operated power tools such as drills, staple guns
- Portable camp stove and fuel
- One fire extinguisher per floor
- Toolkit with pliers, handsaw, duct tape, crowbar, sledgehammer

Clothing:

- Change of clothing and footwear
- Sturdy shoes or work boots
- Thermal underwear
- Rain gear
- Hat and gloves
- Blankets, sleeping bags

Special Items:

- Prescription medications and supplies
- Personal hygiene items
- Toilet paper
- Extra eyeglasses
- Baby supplies
- Garbage bags and ties
- Extra set of house and other keys
- Copies of or a spreadsheet listing insurance policies, credit cards, official identification, bank information
- Copies of other vital documents
- Pet food

Resources for Computer, Internet-Related and Intellectual-Property Crime

Type of Crime	Appropriate Federal Investigative Law Enforcement Agencies
Computer intrusion (i.e., hacking)	FBI local office (www.fbi.gov) U.S. Secret Service (www.treasury.gov) Internet Crime Complaint Center (www.ic3.gov)
Password trafficking	FBI local office (www.fbi.gov) U.S. Secret Service (www.treasury.gov) Internet Crime Complaint Center (www.ic3.gov)
Counterfeiting of currency	U.S. Secret Service (www.treasury.gov)
Child pornography or exploitation	FBI local office (www.fbi.gov) Internet Crime Complaint Center (www.ic3.gov)
Child exploitation and internet fraud matters that have a mail nexus	U.S. Postal Inspection Service (www.usps.com) Internet Crime Complaint Center (www.ic3.gov)
Internet fraud and spam	FBI local office (www.fbi.gov) U.S. Secret Service (Financial Crimes Division) (www.treasury.gov) Federal Trade Commission (www.ftc.gov) If securities-fraud or investment-related spam e-mails: Securities and Exchange Commission (www.sec.gov) Internet Crime Complaint Center (www.ic3.gov)
Internet harassment	FBI local office (www.fbi.gov)
Internet bomb threats	FBI local office (www.fbi.gov) ATF local office (www.atf.gov)

Type of Crime	Appropriate Federal Investigative Law Enforcement Agencies
Trafficking in explosive/ incendiary devices or firearms over the internet	FBI local office (www.fbi.gov) ATF local office (www.atf.gov)

Checklist of Travel Websites

Government Resources
Centers for Disease Control: www.cdc.gov/travel
Smart Traveler Enrollment Program: travelregistration.state.gov
Transportation Security Administration (TSA): www.tsa.gov
U.S. Customs & Border Protection: www.cbp.gov
U.S. Department of State: www.travel.state.gov

Travel Insurance Comparisons
Insure My Trip: www.insuremytrip.com

Other Resources for the Independent Traveler
Lonely Planet: www.lonelyplanet.com
LP Message Board: https://www.lonelyplanet.com/thorntree/
BootsnAll Travel Network: www.bootsnall.com
Rick Steves' Europe Through the Back Door: www.ricksteves.com
New York Times Travel: www.nytimes.com/section/travel
Wall Street Journal, "The Middle Seat":
https://www.wsj.com/news/types/the-middle-seat

Vital Documents
You should keep a collection of documents stored:
- in a waterproof container in your emergency kit
- away from your home
- off-site electronically.

Vital Home Documents

Home and auto policies

Passport

Driver's license

Credit cards

Immunization records

Other medical information, if relevant

Wills and medical directives

Bank-account numbers

Inventory list of investments

Household-goods inventory

Family records (birth and marriage licenses)

═══════════

Vital Work Documents

Your hire letter and any informational material
included from HR

Any performance reviews that you have received

Professional recommendations

Awards, citations, or thank-you notes received from
executives

Any requests or plans for work improvement

Current copy of your résumé or curriculum vitae

List or photos of personal assets in your office or
cubicle in case of loss

Vital Travel Documents

Passport

International driver's license

Debit or credit card(s)

Emergency contact information

Health-insurance card

Travel-insurance document

Doctor's letter to cover any special medical condition

Vital Internet Documents

Bills of sale for computers and other electronic devices, including warranty information and serial numbers, including smart IoT devices you install in your home

License-agreement numbers for such items as anti-virus software or online backup

Copies of purchase agreements on applications, including serial numbers and secure location for storing copies of DVDs/CDs

Annie Searle is the founder and principal at Annie Searle & Associates, a Seattle-based risk research and advisory firm founded in 2009. From 1999 to 2009 Searle worked at Washington Mutual, most of that time as senior executive in charge of enterprise risk services, and as chair of the crisis-management team for six years. Searle is one of the founders and served as president and CEO of Delphi Computers & Peripherals from 1984 to 1999, earning both the "Northwest Entrepreneur of the Year" award from Ernst & Young and Inc. Magazine, and the "Woman of Achievement" award from the Matrix Table. She has two degrees in literature from the University of Iowa. Searle is a senior lecturer in the University of Washington's School of Information, where she has just been awarded the 2019 Teaching Excellence and Creative Honors (TEACH) award. She is a lifetime member of the Institute of American Entrepreneurs; and an inaugural 2011 inductee to the Hall of Fame for Women in Emergency Management and Homeland Security. She is a member of the board of directors of the Seattle Public Library Foundation and a pro bono risk advisor to the Seattle Police Department.

www.ingramcontent.com/pod-product-compliance
Lightning Source LLC
Chambersburg PA
CBHW060608200326
41521CB00007B/694